A Cold Day In Hell

Craig Wallace

Copyright © 2016 Craig Wallace

All rights reserved.

ISBN:
978-1-329-65289-7

DEDICATION

To my beautiful daughters Emily and Erin Flynn and to the memory of my late parents John Patrick Wallace and Barbara Ruth Wallace.

CONTENTS

Dedication iii
Contents v
Acknowledgements vii
Prologue   A Cold Day In Hell ix
Setting the Stage 13
The Santee Sioux Uprising 17
The Conflict Spreads 31
The Bozeman Trail 37
Colonel Henry Carrington 47
Captain William J. Fetterman 53
The Journey West 57
Lieutenant George Grummond 81
Fetterman Arrives 93
Entering Hell 115
Aftermath clv
Bibliography clxiii
About the Author clxv

ACKNOWLEDGEMENTS

A very special thank you to my beautiful, amazing girlfriend Maria Bracalenti who allowed me to drag her out to Wyoming in the summer of 2015, where we experienced the "magnificent desolation" of the Fetterman battlefield and saw the haunting site of Fort Phil Kearny. Maria was with me through thick and thin, from the beginning of this book to the very end. I couldn't have done it with out you and I can't wait for you to be with me through the next book! I love you.

Thanks to my best friend Heidi Dakin and her friend Nicole Witkowski for my front and back covers. These two ladies are amazing artists! If any reader wants some great art work produced contact me and I will put you in touch with Heidi and Nicole!

Thank you as well to Nick Cheng for his invaluable assistance in formatting this book.

As well I need to acknowledge an error I made in my previous book "Into the Valley of Death." When I briefly wrote about the Fetterman battle in that book I made the error of only relying on the most common descriptions of the battle. I failed to thoroughly research the subject and thus my description of the Fetterman battle in that book is incorrect. I am setting the story straight in this book and I hope have helped to bring honor to Captain William Fetterman and his family.

PROLOGUE

A COLD DAY IN HELL

Friday December 21, 1866, 11:00am Local Time

Fort Phil Kearny,

Mountain District, Wyoming Territory

Colonel Henry Carrington bolted out of his office chair at the shouts from the sentries posted on the stockade walls.

"Pickets report the wood train under attack", the sentries called out.

Carrington burst outside and looked towards Pilot Hill, where he had established permanent pickets to provide warning to the fort in case of hostile Indian attacks, which usually occurred on a daily basis. The pickets were waving flags in a motion indicating that the party of men who had ventured outside to cut wood for the fort were under attack by Sioux and Cheyenne warriors. From far off came the sound of gunfire as the military escorts protecting the wood train began firing on attacking Sioux and Cheyenne warriors.

"Oh my lord," Carrington thought. "Could those red devils not give us just one day of peace? Even just a few quiet hours to cut some wood?"

As the colonel came outside, Captain James Powell came running forward. He saluted and exclaimed, "The wood train has been attacked, sir!"

"Take command of a detachment, Captain Powell," ordered the colonel, "and drive those hostiles away. You will simply relieve the wood train. Do not follow the hostiles and invite any unnecessary engagement. Do exactly what you did two days ago."

"Yes, sir." Powell saluted and ran towards the stables.

As soon as Powell headed towards the stables, Captain William J. Fetterman approached Colonel Carrington.

"Colonel, I respectfully request command of the relief column sir," Fetterman stated.

Carrington looked nervously at Fetterman. The two men had an uneasy relationship, to say the least. Fetterman was a highly decorated combat veteran of the Civil War, while Carrington had spent the Civil War in administrative duties. Fetterman, since arriving at Fort Phil Kearny in early November 1866, had been urging Carrington to take offensive action against the Sioux and Cheyenne. It seemed as if every day the hostiles were attacking the various wood cutting parties. In Fetterman's mind, the failure of the army to go out and strike the hostiles in response was a sign of sheer cowardice. He was positive the soldiers could and would inflict a major defeat upon the hostiles – if only they were given an opportunity to do so. Carrington, however, was concerned about his small force of soldiers and the meager amounts of ammunition he had on hand. He had repeatedly declined Fetterman's "advice." Now he felt his back was against the wall.

"Captain Fetterman, on what basis do you make your request?" Carrington asked. (He, in fact, knew what answer would be forthcoming.

"Colonel, as you are well aware, my brevet rank[1] was Colonel. I thus claim command of the column due to outranking Captain Powell. Sir," Fetterman stated firmly.

Carrington knew he had no basis to deny Fetterman's request. Fetterman had every right to request command of the column based on his brevet rank, and to receive it. Carrington also knew that most of the officers stationed at Fort Phil Kearny were viewing him with contempt due to his reluctance to strike out at the warriors tormenting the fort. Captain William J. Fetterman was a highly decorated officer of the Civil War. He was a born combat officer. If anyone under his command could whip the savages, it would be Fetterman. Carrington thus decided to "roll the dice" and turn Fetterman loose.

"Very well Captain, the command of the relief column is yours. But listen closely. You have pushed me to allow you a chance to punish these savages. Now you have your chance. Don't put your command into a situation where you will be heavily outnumbered, as I don't have much relief that I can send to you. But if you can hit them - hit them hard. Am I clear?"

Captain Fetterman looked at Carrington closely. For a moment he was stunned. He didn't respect his commanding officer and he was

---

1 In this time period, US officers could receive temporary or "brevet" promotions to a higher rank. This was usually based on a superb combat record. When peacetime came, they were reduced in rank to that of their "normal" rank. However social protocol at the time dictated that an officer would be referred to by the highest rank they had achieved.

"itching" for a battle with the hostiles. He didn't think Carrington would ever "take the leash off of him." But Carrington had done so and now he clearly had his chance.

"Your orders are very clear Colonel. I will carry them out."

With that, Fetterman dashed towards his quarters to gather his personal weapons. The firing from the wood train was growing more intense, adding a sense of urgency to his stride. As he reached his quarters his long-time friend, Quartermaster Captain Frederick (Fred) Brown, hurried up to him and said:

"Will, I am coming with you. I still have a score to settle with those red bastards. And I am not leaving around here until I take Red Cloud's scalp." [2]

Captain Fetterman responded as he went through his door, "That's fine, Fred. We are leaving quickly, so get your rifle and meet me at the main gates. I can use you out there. And Fred: Carrington just gave us our hunting license."

Captain Fred Brown looked at his friend in shock. Like Fetterman, he felt Carrington was timid – basically a coward. But now he and Fetterman would get their chance.

Fetterman knew that today he was going to get his chance to show Carrington just how hostile Indians were best dealt with. Those hostiles would "rue the day" that they decided to provoke the United States Army under the command of Captain William J. Fetterman into battle!

---

[2] Captain Brown had been ordered to a new duty station, and was due to depart Fort Phil Kearny within a few weeks, weather permitting.

SETTING THE STAGE

The roots of the events of December 21, 1866, were planted years earlier. Across the modern Great Plains states and Prairie provinces of Canada lived and roamed the nomadic members of the mighty Sioux Nation. The Sioux are made up of three major linguistically and regionally based groups and several subgroups. The groups are:

Lakota (a.k.a. Lakȟóta, Teton)

Western Dakota (a.k.a. Yankton-Yanktonai or Dakȟóta)

Eastern Dakota (a.k.a. Santee-Sisseton or Dakhóta)

These groups were further divided into sub-tribal groups such as (but not limited to):

Oglala

Hunkpapa

Minniconjou

Sans Arc

Two Kettle

Santee

Blackfoot

Brule

Initially, as white settlers streamed across the plains the Sioux tried to avoid them. Most of the whites were simply heading to the gold fields of California and had no interest in Sioux land, outside of getting across it. The Sioux who were nomadic simply let them through.

However, as time went on, more and more whites began settling on the Great Plains and as a result began encroaching into what the Sioux considered "their land." In an effort to avoid hostilities, the United States government sent treaty commissioners to meet with the Sioux and other Great Plains Indians such as the Cheyenne, Arapaho, Crow, Assiniboine, Mandan, Hidatsa, and Arikara. (The Crow and Arikara were traditional enemies of the Sioux.) On September 17, 1851, the first Treaty of Fort Laramie was signed between the United States government and the Sioux, Cheyenne, Arapaho, Assiniboine, Mandan, Hidastsa and Arikara nations. (The Crow did not sign the treaty.) The Indian nations guaranteed safe passage for settlers across their land in return for promises of an annuity in the amount of fifty thousand dollars for fifty years and that the U.S. government would discourage the creation of white settlements on Indian land. The Indian nations also allowed roads and forts to be built in their territories.

This treaty kept the peace for several years until the Pikes Peak Gold Rush began in 1858. This gold rush created a massive "rush" of settlers and emigrants across the Great Plains and into the Indian nation's territory as detailed in the 1851 Fort Laramie Treaty. Many of those same settlers decided to settle on lands that the Treaty clearly identified as Indian territory. When the Indians protested this mass "invasion" of their lands, the U.S. government made the decision not to enforce the terms of the Treaty. The Plains Indians had just received a hard lesson on how seriously Washington took the treaties they signed with Indian nations.

The first reported clash between Sioux warriors and US Army soldiers came on August 19, 1854. On that day a small detachment of 29 soldiers commanded by Lieutenant John Grattan rode into a Brule

Sioux village, located just east of Fort Laramie in modern- day Wyoming. The soldiers had arrived in response to a complaint by a Mormon wagon train that the Sioux had stolen and butchered one of their cows. A preliminary investigation by the military officials and the fort's Indian Agent indicated that a Sioux warrior by the name of High Forehead was guilty of this crime. The army attempted to negotiate with local chief Conquering Bear to have High Forehead turned over to the army for trial. Conquering Bear declared that he had no power to do this, and instead offered the Mormons compensation of one of his prize horses. He was trying to avoid hostilities. His offer, however, was declined, and the army then decided to assert their authority by arresting High Forehead in his village.

Lieutenant Grattan, upon entering the village, began speaking through an interpreter, Luciene Auguste (who unbeknownst to Grattan, was despised by the Sioux, and who was drinking heavily all day leading up to this), to Conquering Bear. He was trying to ascertain where High Forehead was. As the discussion stretched on, tempers among the soldiers and warriors became frayed. There were over 1,200 warriors in the village, and the soldiers were quickly becoming very nervous. They realized that if a battle broke out here they were going to lose. Grattan had by now realized that Auguste was completely intoxicated, and he grabbed a bottle from Auguste's hand and smashed it against his own saddle. By now mounted Sioux warriors were beginning to gallop around the nervous soldiers shouting insults. Auguste, in response, began calling the Sioux warriors "women" and loudly declaring that the soldiers had arrived to fight, not to talk.

Perhaps if Grattan had gained control of Auguste right here, and retreated from the village, the situation may have been saved. Instead, with Auguste baiting the Sioux and the young warriors riding around the now terrified soldiers, the inevitable occurred. A soldier fired, killing Conquering Bear. Almost instantly the Sioux returned fire.

Grattan's troops desperately tried to defend themselves. However, the small group of soldiers was impaled by swarms of arrows. Calling this a "battle" would be charitable. The soldiers were wiped out within minutes. There were no survivors.

When word of the "massacre" of Lieutenant Grattan's command reached Washington, revenge was swift and brutal. Brigadier General William S. Harney led a large detachment of troops that found and quickly destroyed a large force of Sioux in Nebraska the following year.

Tensions continued to run high across the Great Plains for the next seven years, until the outbreak of the Civil War. At that point, the U.S. government diverted the vast majority of its military might to fighting the Southern rebels and trying to restore the union

THE SANTEE SIOUX UPRISING

Washington returned its attention to the Great Plain and the Sioux in 1862 in, of all states, Minnesota. That northern state always had a peaceful reputation. The majority of "clashes" between whites and the Sioux and Cheyenne usually came in the modern-day states of North and South Dakota, Wyoming, Montana, and Nebraska, among others. Minnesota seemed like a "peaceful backwater." There the Santee Sioux, led by Chief Little Crow, had agreed to move to a reservation near Fort Ridgely in the southwestern portion of the state. As part of the agreement to move to the reservation, the U.S. government had agreed to feed the Sioux. In this case, unlike other government "boondoggles," Washington had properly allocated funds to buy the necessary rations. However, the payments were late in reaching the reservation agent who was responsible for the administration of the reservation. (The late payment was really a reflection of transportation challenges of that era. The money had to be sent in the form of gold, and it took time to physically transport a large shipment of gold across primitive roads, railways, etc.)

On August 15, 1862, Sioux representatives appealed to Agent Andrew Myrick, who was responsible for the distribution of supplies at the Lower Agency (part of the overall reservation), to please release the supplies that he had stored in warehouses. Myrick refused to release the food to the Sioux until payment arrived. The Sioux, who were not allowed to hunt their own food, were starving. They pointed out that just two weeks earlier at the Upper Agency, the agent there had released food to the Sioux "on credit" while he awaited payment from Washington. (The agent at the Upper Agency was fearful that violence would break out if he failed to release the supplies.) Myrick would not listen to reason. In fact, he publicly commented "So far as I am concerned, if they are hungry, let them eat grass." Unbeknownst to those gathered at the Lower Agency, the payments were on their way to the Minnesota agency. On August 16, a keg with $71,000 worth of gold coins reached St. Paul. The next day the keg was sent to Fort Ridgely for distribution to the Dakota. It arrived a few hours too late as the Sioux reacted with an unprecedented rage against the late payments and the attitude of Andrew Myrick.

On August 17th, a small group of Sioux warriors raided a farm near the Lower Agency while looking for eggs. They killed five people, including a teenage girl. When the warriors responsible for the attack rode into the reservation, they told Little Crow what they had done. He listened carefully, and then announced that the whites would never forgive the killing of these farmers, especially the killing of a young girl. It was best that the Sioux strike the whites now - and hard - before they could fully mobilize.

When Little Crow called for war, he found his warriors eager. They attacked the agency and slaughtered every white they could find. Agent Myrick's body was found full of arrows and his mouth stuffed with grass. The great Santee Sioux uprising of 1862 had begun.

Two days later, on August 19, 1862, Little Crow's warriors attacked the village of New Ulm. Approximately 100 Sioux warriors opened fire on the village from bluffs that surrounded the village. The villagers barricaded themselves in their homes and many returned fire. A long-range battle raged through the day until heavy thunderstorms rolled in and the Sioux retreated. Six settlers were killed in that first day of fighting, and five were wounded.

As word of the battle spread, state authorities rushed troops, under the command of Colonel Henry Hastings Sibley, to New Ulm as fear of another attack was rampant. About 300 poorly armed and trained state militia (an early form of the modern National Guard) arrived in

New Ulm. They moved into the village as the settlers there frantically tried to improve their fortifications. The soldiers quickly began work on fortifications of their own as they braced for what they felt was an impending attack. They dug trenches, and cut holes in the walls of homes and businesses to use as firing slits. They were prepared for a momentous battle, one that they knew would allow for no mercy by either side.

As soldiers prepared New Ulm for a new assault upon it, the Sioux attacked Fort Ridgely on August 20. A bloody two-day battle then occurred, with the Sioux launching numerous assaults against the fort only to be driven back by determined soldiers.

At about 9:30 am on Saturday, August 23, approximately 1,000 Sioux resumed their attack on New Ulm. They encircled the village, pouring heavy fire from rifles, muskets, and bows and arrows into the village. The beleaguered defenders of the village returned fire as best they could. Soldiers and civilians fought side by side desperately trying to protect their families, comrades, and homes. The air was thick with heavy black smoke from the guns of both sides, the screams of terrified settlers, shrieks of pain from the wounded soldiers and warriors, and orders bellowed from officers and sergeants. The Sioux war cries were bone-chilling to the white soldiers and civilians. As the warriors closed in on the village, the soldiers and civilians poured gunfire into them and then retreated, setting fire to buildings as they did so. As they ignited the buildings, the soldiers and civilians would fall back to their next line of defense. The burning buildings added a layer of defense that the Sioux would have to try to fight their way through. The fighting raged until nightfall, when the Sioux pulled back. All night civilian and army surgeons worked desperately in primitive conditions to save the wounded. Buildings and fortifications blazed in a scene that seemed right out of Dante's Inferno.

As the doctors fought their battles to save the wounded, many families in the village had grim conversations. Wives and husbands huddled in their barricaded homes and discussed the nightmare possibility. What if the Sioux broke through the soldier's defenses and got into the town? What would their fate be? Or in particular, the fate of the women and children? The consensus seemed to be that in such a situation, the men would be slaughtered, the women raped and probably murdered, and the children either murdered or carried off to live in Sioux villages. The decision by most families was the same. In such a horrific situation, the men would fight as long as possible and then when all was lost, kill their wives and children. Better instant death then a "fate worse than death," as Victorian age women viewed rape and the loss of their children. The modern reader can only imagine the horror of such discussions and the planning for such an event. Little sleep was to be had in New Ulm that night.

Luckily for the citizens of New Ulm, such a situation did not materialize. The following morning, numerous Sioux warriors fired long range shots into the village and then simply withdrew. It appeared that they didn't relish the massive casualties they would incur by storming the barricaded village. The total casualties for the soldiers and settlers was 34 killed and 60 wounded. Fully 1/3 of the town had been destroyed. The Sioux casualties are unknown, as the Sioux would almost always carry their dead and wounded away from the battlefield. It is assumed by historians that Sioux casualties were very high in this battle. The soldiers and the citizens of New Ulm had put up a defense that any modern army general would deeply respect.

Two days later, upon pleas from military officials, the remaining residents of New Ulm abandoned the smoking ruins of their town. There was no guarantee that the Sioux would not be back, and the small military forces in Minnesota simply could not be tied down there.

For the next two weeks, Little Crow's warriors struck at will across the state. Farms and villages were burned to the ground, and settlers were slaughtered. The public was in an uproar. Many felt that while their government may be guilty of some negative actions directed towards the Sioux, what did that have to do with innocent settlers – and in particular women and children? Why did they have to be slaughtered by the Sioux due to political errors? And to add to the horror, the small number of US Army troops and Minnesota militia seemed helpless to protect their citizens.

On August 31, 1862, Colonel Sibley, who had commanded the military forces at the second battle of New Ulm and at Fort Ridgely, sent out a detachment of about 170 soldiers commanded by Major Joseph Brown from Fort Ridgely. Their orders were to bury the bodies of settlers who had been massacred by Little Crow's warriors in the vicinity of the fort. On September 1, these forces camped near Birch Coulee, in what is now Renville County, Minnesota. Major Brown was completely unaware that a force of over 200 Sioux warriors had been tracking his column and was now prepared to strike.

At dawn the next day, September 2, the Sioux attacked Major Brown's camp. Within minutes, over 30 cavalry troopers were lying dead or wounded along with most of their horses. The soldiers fought back desperately, pumping gunfire into the swarming masses of Sioux. By now, the camp was completely encircled and Major Brown was convinced his command was in mortal danger.

Back at Fort Ridgely, 16 miles away, Colonel Sibley heard the far-off sounds of heavy firing. He ordered Colonel Samuel McPhail to lead a relief column, made up of 240 troopers, to aid Major Brown. As McPhail's forces closed in on Birch Coulee, they were attacked by a large group of Sioux led by Chief Grey Bird. Instead of attempting to advance through the Sioux, as some cavalry officers such as George Armstrong Custer would have done, McPhail halted his advance and briefly retreated. He then stopped the retreat and formed skirmish lines. [3] As his men opened fire on Grey Bird's warriors, McPhail sent Lieutenant Timothy Sheehan (who had played a prominent role in the defense of Fort Ridgely only weeks earlier) back to the fort to inform Colonel Sibley of the situation. Sheehan leaned low over his horse and rode as "if he was pursued by demons" back to Fort Ridgely. Upon receiving the updated situation report from Lieutenant Sheehan, Colonel Sibley rushed more cavalry reinforcements plus an artillery brigade under his own personal command to McPhail's rescue. He ordered the artillery to fire on the Sioux, and the shells which came exploding in amongst them convinced Little Crow and his followers that it would be judicious to retreat. This relieved Colonel McPhail and Major Brown and resulted in the survival of the majority of their forces. That being said, the Sioux had scored a decisive victory over the army at Birch Coulee.

By now the State of Minnesota was in a collective state of terror. The Sioux seemed to be everywhere, poised to strike anyplace in the state. Governor Alexander Ramsay appealed to Washington for assistance. President Abraham Lincoln was furious at the news in Minnesota. With the Civil War engulfing his nation in an absolute "blood bath," the last thing he needed was a major war with the Sioux. That being said, Lincoln had to respond.

He created the Department of the Northwest on September 6, 1862. He then ordered General John Pope to take command of the department and to crush the Sioux.

General John Pope was a very experienced officer. He had good

---

[3] A skirmish line is a standard cavalry defensive formation. Upon the order to "form skirmishers," men break into predetermined groups of four. One, who is assigned to be the horse holder, takes the reins of his and the other three horses and retreats to any area of safety. The other three troopers kneel on a line about five yards apart and fight from that position.

success fighting the Confederates in the Western Theater and was given command of the Union Army of Virginia by President Lincoln and ordered to the Eastern theater of operations. The President was desperate to find an aggressive Union General who could match not only the aggressiveness of Confederate Generals such as Robert E. Lee and Thomas J. (Stonewall) Jackson, but could also match their skill and courage. Lincoln hoped Pope would be his man.

Pope began by quickly alienating the majority of his subordinates by denigrating their past performance against the Southern rebels while boasting of his own accomplishments. In very short order his men — whom he would need to have any success against the Confederates - despised him.

The first test he faced with his new command came at the First Battle of Rappahannock Station on August 22-25, 1862. On that first day rebel cavalry forces under the command of legendary Confederate General J.E.B. Stuart raided Pope's headquarters, almost capturing the new Union General. Over the next few days, Pope's forces retreated under a massive onslaught from Stonewall Jackson's forces. By August 25, Jackson's forces were destroying Union supply depots far to the rear of Pope's command. So far, Pope's move to the "Eastern Theater" looked like it had been a disaster.

Three days later, it would become known as the Second Battle of Bull Run (known to Southern sympathizers as "The Second Battle of Manassas") General John Pope received a second opportunity to prove to Lincoln that he was the right man for the job.

Pope's forces had retreated after the Battle of Rappahannock Station towards their supply depot at Manassas Station that had been destroyed by Stonewall Jackson's forces. Jackson in return had retreated a few miles to the northwest. Pope now became convinced that he had trapped Jackson and decided to destroy his tormentor. On August 29, Pope launched a series of savage attacks against

Jackson's position. The attacks were repulsed with heavy casualties on both sides. At noon, Confederate General James Longstreet was ordered into action by General Robert E. Lee, the overall commander of the Confederate Army of Northern Virginia. Longstreet's forces smashed through light Union resistance and moved into position on Jackson's right flank. Pope seemed completely unaware of the arrival of the forces of General Longstreet.

On August 30, Pope renewed his attacks on Jackson's dug-in troops. He ordered Major General Fitz John Porter to launch a massive attack, which was quickly devastated by a massive Confederate artillery barrage. As Porter's men fled the battlefield in disarray, Longstreet's command of over 25,000 men counterattacked, in the largest mass assault of the war. Pope's left flank "went to pieces" and his army was quickly in confused, wholescale retreat. It now appeared that Washington, D.C., itself was in danger of being captured by Robert E. Lee's forces. Luckily for the Union, Pope's rear guard fought furiously and were able to slow down the rebel advance enough for more Union forces to arrive to defend the nation's capital.

The defeat of General John Pope and the Union at Second Bull Run was massive. Even though the Union forces outnumbered the Confederate forces 62,000-50,000 they had been severely "whipped." Pope's command had suffered approximately 10,000 dead and wounded, compared to 1,300 dead and 7,000 wounded on the Confederate side. Pope, by all accounts, had been outthought, outmaneuvered, and outfought by his Confederate opponents. After this fiasco, Pope was relieved of his command by President Lincoln.

Less than two weeks later, however, Pope was back in command of an army. President Lincoln's best officers were involved in the Civil War. Pope had proven to be a major disaster there so Lincoln sent him out west to deal with the Sioux. It was a way to get Pope "out of

Lincoln's hair," and perhaps he would serve some useful purpose fighting the Sioux. Pope, embarrassed by his failures just weeks before, arrived on the scene and publicly declared his goal: to drive the Sioux right out of Minnesota.

Before Pope could fully take command however, the tide turned quickly against Little Crow and the Sioux. On September 19, Colonel Sibley's troops, encouraged by General Pope, left Fort Ridgely seeking their enemy.

Three days later, on September 22, Sibley's forces were camped on the shores of Battle Lake. (The upcoming battle would strangely become known as the "Battle of Wood Lake," which was actually located three miles away.) That night, a large force of Sioux warriors, who had been tracking the progress of Sibley's column, moved down from their camp which was located near the Chippewa River and moved into position near Sibley's encampment. Their plan was to take cover over night and launch a massive unexpected attack the next day as the soldiers just began to break camp and move out.

The battle began, almost by accident. A group of Sibley's men set out from the camp seeking more food. As they moved across the prairie, the soldiers surprised a group of Sioux warriors who were hidden in the foliage near Sibley's camp.

The warriors sprang from their hiding places and the troopers responded with a barrage of gunfire. The firing roused the remainder of Sibley's men who frantically grabbed their weapons, rushed from their tents and headed for their mounts. They poured out of their camp and headed for the sounds of the firing.

Within about two hours, the battle was over. The badly outnumbered Sioux had finally succumbed to Sibley's superior numbers and firepower and were thoroughly defeated. It was also noted after the engagement that Colonel Sibley and his officers had done a magnificent job directing their forces in the battle.

Some firsthand accounts of the Battle of Wood Lake have survived to this day. One of those was provided by Wamditanka (Jerome Big Eagle), a Sioux who led fighters into battle against Sibley's troops.

"We expected to throw the whole white force into confusion by a sudden and unexpected attack," Wamditanka later recalled. "I think this was a good plan of battle. Our concealed men would not have been discovered. The grass was tall and the place by the road and the ravine were good hiding places. The morning came and an accident spoiled our plans. For some reason Sibley did not move early, as we expected. It seemed a considerable time after sun-up when four or five wagons with a number of soldiers started out from the camp in the direction of the old Yellow Medicine Agency. They came on over the prairie, right where part of our line was. Some of the wagons were not on the road, and if they had kept straight on would have driven right over where our men were as they lay in the grass. At last they came so close that our men had to rise up and fire. This brought on the fight, of course, but not according to the way we had planned it. Little Crow saw it and felt very badly."

Over the next week, Sibley accepted the surrender of close to 2,000 Sioux. Many other Sioux fled north into Dakota Territory and up into Canada. Little Crow fled into what would later become the Canadian province of Manitoba. If he stayed in Canada, he was safe from the vengeance of the United States Government and its army.

Little Crow had good reason to stay away from the United States. On September 28, 1862, Colonel Sibley appointed a military commission to "try summarily" Sioux for "murder and other outrages" committed against Americans. Sibley knew the American people, and in particular the people of Minnesota, wanted revenge. Hopefully, the upcoming trials would give them this revenge. Whether Sibley had authority to appoint such a commission is a matter of substantial dispute. (It probably should have been ordered by General Pope and approved by the President.)

The military commission or tribunal was convened quickly. Sixteen trials were conducted the first day at Camp Release, Minnesota resulting in convictions and death sentences for ten prisoners and acquittals for another six. (The high number of acquittals certainly seemed to indicate to Sibley's credit that these were no "kangaroo court" sessions. That impression would soon change.) Over the six weeks, the military court would try a total of 393 cases, convicting 323. Of the 323 convictions, 303 resulted in death sentences.

The military commission openly declared that "mere participation" in a battle justified a death sentence. If a prisoner admitted firing shots in battle then a guilty verdict quickly followed.

Somewhat more time and deliberation was required for trials in which the charge was the murder or rape of settlers, as warriors were not nearly as quick to plead guilty in such cases. After the defendant gave his testimony, prosecution witnesses were summoned. When prosecution witnesses contradicted the testimony of the defendant, the commission would usually find the prisoner to be guilty.

Since then, many legal and historical critics have challenged the fairness of the trials. In addition to raising concerns about the sufficiency of the evidence supporting convictions and the speed of trials, these same critics have charged commission members of being biased against the defendants. The critics may have a point. The commission members, though men of honor and integrity, were also officers whose troops had fought these same defendants. The reader should ask "could one be a fair judge in these same circumstances"?

Colonel Sibley, however, knew the people of Minnesota wanted revenge. He may well have viewed rapid summary trials by a military commission as necessary to avoid vigilante justice by angry mobs of

Minnesotans. The American people were not interested in "true justice" at this point in time in Minnesota.

If this was the case, Sibley was proven correct on November 9, 1862, as the 303 condemned were attacked by a mob in New Ulm, Minnesota (site of two furious battles only months before) as they were being transported to Mankato, Minnesota, to await their execution. The guards surrounding the condemned prisoners put up a furious battle that resulted in the mob being driven off. The military guards then thwarted yet another attempted attack by vigilantes on the condemned weeks later.

The final decision on whether to go ahead with the mass execution of the 303 Sioux warriors lay with President Lincoln. General John Pope urged the President by telegraph to approve the speedy execution of all the condemned. Virtually all of the citizens of Minnesota agreed with Pope.

One of the few citizens of Minnesota who did not agree with the executions was the Episcopal Bishop of Minnesota, Henry Whipple. He traveled to Washington to meet with the President and his advisors to discuss the causes of the Santee Sioux uprising. Whipple made a well-reasoned, articulate plea on behalf of the condemned. President Lincoln was a well-regarded lawyer in his own right, and the visit by Whipple impressed and moved him deeply. Lincoln pledged to reform Indian affairs. He was well aware of the shortcoming of his own governments' Indian policies and practices. However, Lincoln also knew that the lust for Sioux blood in Minnesota could not be ignored. If he was to commute the executions, the likely result would be mobs storming the prison where the condemned were being held, and a resulting massacre of the prisoners, guards, and rampaging citizens. Lincoln thus asked two of the government's legal clerks to go through the commission's trial records and identify those prisoners convicted of raping women or children and killing settlers. The clerks found 39 who had been convicted of these crimes. President Lincoln at that point agreed that the execution of those 39 would proceed.

On December 26, 1862, 38 Sioux were hung (an additional warrior had been pardoned before this date after additional evidence had been obtained) at Mankato, Minnesota. To date, it is the largest mass execution in American history.

By heading to Canada, Little Crow had escaped the "hang man." However, he would soon make a decision that would cost him his life. He decided that the Sioux had been robbed of their land, and so he returned to the United States to steal horses from whites in Minnesota. On the evening of July 3, 1863, while he and his son Wowinapa were foraging for raspberries in a clearing in the Big Woods, they were spotted by two farmers, Nathan Lamson and his son Chauncey. The four engaged in a brief exchange of gunfire where Little Crow wounded Nathan Lamson. The elder Lamson and his son then returned fire, mortally wounding Little Crow. Before dying, Little Crow convinced his son to flee. The Lamsons, sure there were more Sioux in the area, fled nearly 12 miles to Hutchinson, Minnesota to raise the alarm. The following day, a search party arrived at the scene to find an unidentified dead Sioux man. (The body would later be identified as that of Little Crow.) The body wore a coat belonging to a white settler murdered two days before. The members of the search party, remembering the blood bath of the previous year, were furious. They first scalped Little Crow. Later the entire body itself was brought back to Hutchinson. Little Crow's corpse was dragged down the town's main street while firecrackers were placed in his ears and nose. The body was then decapitated and tossed into a pit at a slaughterhouse.

On July 28, 1863, his son Wowinapa was captured by troops in the vicinity of Devil's Lake, Dakota Territory. Upon capture, he informed the soldiers of the death of his father near Hutchison. That prompted an exhumation of the body on August 16 1863. Little

Crow's identity was verified by the scarred and malformed wrists. Little Crow was viewed by residents of Minnesota in the same manner Westerners viewed Osama Bin Laden after September 11, 2001. The news of his death prompted sighs of great relief across the state and led to a large financial reward for Nathan Lamson.

The bloodshed wasn't quite over. After the defeat of the Sioux at Wood Lake and the resulting executions, some refugees and warriors made their way to modern day North and South Dakota (known as Dakota Territory at the time.) Battles continued between the forces of the Department of the Northwest commanded by General John Pope and Sioux through 1863 and into 1864. Colonel Henry Sibley, operating under Pope, and with over 2,000 men, pursued the Sioux into Dakota Territory. Sibley's troops defeated the Sioux in four major battles in less than two months in 1863: the Battle of Big Mound on July 24, 1863; the Battle of Dead Buffalo Lake just days late on July 26, 1863; the Battle of Stony Lake two days after that, and finally the Battle of Whitestone Hill on September 3, 1863. The Sioux retreated further west, but again clashed with U.S. military forces in 1864. In this case, General Alfred Sully commanded a force from near Fort Pierre in modern-day South Dakota, and soundly defeated the Sioux at the Battle of Killdeer Mountain on July 28, 1864.

With Sully's victory the Sioux moved west towards the modern-day states of Wyoming and Montana, trying to avoid the rapidly encroaching white settlers. And the United States Army had proven to itself that it had the ability to "whip" the Sioux when necessary.

THE CONFLICT SPREADS

Colorado Territory (now modern-day Colorado) during the 1850's and 1860's was a place of phenomenal growth. There were numerous gold and silver rushes. Miners by the tens of thousands had "poured" into the area seeking to make their fortunes. Their appearance had infuriated the Cheyenne and Arapahos in the area. The Pike's Peak Gold Rush in 1858 brought the tension in this area to a boiling point. The 1851 Fort Laramie Treaty had designated this area as Indian Territory. However, whites were not going to allow the presence of a treaty to keep them away from gold!

Washington opened up negotiations with the Arapaho and Cheyenne, and in February 1861 10 chiefs from these tribes signed the Treaty of Fort Wise with the United States government. This treaty drastically shrunk the area of land originally "given" to the Indians in the 1851 Fort Laramie Treaty. The signing of this treaty outraged hundreds of Cheyenne and Arapaho, and they disavowed it. (In Native American culture, chiefs had moral authority, but no legal authority, and thus had no way to enforce the terms of any treaty they had signed). As a result, war broke out. Throughout 1863 and into 1864, Cheyenne and Arapaho warriors savagely attacked wagon trains, mining camps, farms, and stagecoach lines. As in Minnesota two years earlier, the military garrisons in this region were reduced by the Civil War, so settlers could not count on protection from the army.

Governor John Evans decided to take a hard line against these Indian attacks. He had no interest at all in any point of view raised by the Indians in their defense. He wanted them hurt, and hurt badly. He ordered Colonel John Chivington to take the First Regiment of Colorado Volunteers and strike hard against the Cheyenne and Arapaho.

In Evans' eyes, John Chivington was just the man for the job. A Methodist minister, he had declined Evans offer to be commissioned as a Chaplain in the Colorado Volunteers during the Civil War, as Chivington wanted to fight. Against the Confederates, he proved to be a very capable soldier, winning a series of victories and leading his men very effectively. As well, Chivington, despite being a religious minister, had almost a "pathological hatred" of Indians. Author Dee Brown, in his 1970 book "Bury My Heart at Wounded Knee," quoted Chivington as saying:

"Damn any man who sympathizes with Indians! ... I have come to kill Indians, and believe it is right and honorable to use any means under God's heaven to kill Indians. ... Kill and scalp all, big and little; nits make lice." [4]

Chivington's soldiers started attacking and destroying Cheyenne camps, the largest of which included about 70 lodges (about 10% of the housing capacity of the entire Cheyenne nation) beginning in April 1864. On May 16, 1864, under orders from Chivington, a force led by Lieutenant George S. Eayre crossed into Kansas and encountered a large group of Cheyenne in their summer buffalo-hunting camp at Big Bushes near the Smoky Hill River. Concerned about the well-being of their families, Cheyenne chiefs Lean Bear and Star approached the soldiers to "parlay" or talk peace. Chivington's men had no interest in peace with Indians. The soldiers opened fire, killing the two chiefs. This in turn enraged the Cheyenne, and promptly started a fresh war between the whites and Cheyenne – this time in Kansas.

In the fall of 1864, Cheyenne chief Black Kettle, desperate to end the fighting, approached the military in Colorado and asked for peace.

---

[4] Brown, Dee, *Bury My Heart at Wounded Knee*, New York, Washington Square Books, 1970, page 85.

He was told by military officials to take his people and make camp close to an area known as Sand Creek (near the military post at Fort Lyon.) While in camp there, he was told to fly an American flag so any troops encountering his camp would know it was peaceful.

Colonel Chivington, however, wasn't going to allow something as "trivial" as a promise by the army to hold him and his troops back. On the night of November 28, 1864, Chivington led a force of over 700 troops towards Black Kettle's camp. They quietly surrounded the village, moved four howitzers into place, and then spent the night drinking heavily in anticipation of the victory that they knew would be up-coming in the morning.

At first light, Chivington, mounted like all his men, raised his arm and then quickly dropped it. The howitzers thundered into action sending explosive shells screaming into the sleeping village. The soldiers spurred their horses, drew sabers and revolvers, and charged the village. Some soldiers unlimbered ropes, and galloped towards the village with the ropes swinging between two mounted cavalry troopers. The idea was that, as they entered the village, the soldiers would charge a tepee, one on either side. The rope would strike the teepee, tearing it away from the ground and exposing the occupants to attack.

Sleeping Cheyenne men, women, and children awoke to exploding shells raining down on them. Warriors sprang from their blankets, frantically grabbed weapons and leapt from their teepees, prepared to fight to the death to defend their families.

It was a fruitless attempt by the warriors. By the time they emerged from their teepees, the soldiers were among them, firing revolvers and carbines,[5] swinging sabers and knocking teepees from their

---

[5] A carbine is a smaller model rifle carried by a cavalry trooper. The longer infantry rifles are simply too cumbersome to be easily used on horseback.

mounts. Chivington's men, fueled by whiskey and the stories of the Sioux depravations in Minnesota two years ago, were in a blood soaked frenzy. The sleepy warriors peered through the smoke and screams looking for targets. Before most of them had any success, they were killed by a soldier's bullet or decapitated by a swinging saber. Indian women, clutching their children desperately ran for safety only, in most cases, to be shot or slashed to death by a soldier swinging a razor-sharp saber.

There was one "bright spot" amongst Chivington's troops at Sand Creek that morning. Captain Silas Soule was commanding Company D of the 1st Colorado Cavalry. Captain Soule was horrified at the Chivington's orders and the resulting bloodshed. He refused to allow his troops to join the "battle" and, along with Lieutenant Joseph Cramer, ordered his men not to fire on civilians. They could protect themselves if attacked but he would not allow his company to get involved in what he considered "cold blooded murder." Soule, in a letter to his former commanding officer and close friend Edward Wynkoop, described what he witnessed:

"I refused to fire, and swore that none but a coward would, for by this time hundreds of women and children were coming towards us, and getting on their knees for mercy. I tell you Ned it was hard to see little children on their knees have their brains beat out by men professing to be civilized. ... I saw two Indians hold one of another's hands, chased until they were exhausted, when they kneeled down, and clasped each other around the neck and were both shot together. They were all scalped, and as high as half a dozen taken from one head. They were all horribly mutilated. One woman was cut open and a child taken out of her, and scalped. ... Squaw's snatches were cut out for trophies. You would think it impossible for white men to butcher and mutilate human beings as they did there." 6

This wasn't a battle. It was a wholesale massacre – cold blooded murder. Men, women, and children were slaughtered. Amidst the bloodshed, Black Kettle's American flag flew forlornly on.

The majority of the village was wiped out. (Chivington lost approximately 10 dead and 30 wounded.) At Chivington's urging, the soldiers then began mutilating the dead. The soldiers cut the heads, breasts and genitals off dead women and men. Dead Indian women were "scalped" of their pubic hair to the loud drunken guffaws of the troopers. Babies had their skulls smashed into "mush" by rifle butts. The remaining standing teepees were ignited. Colonel John Chivingtom beamed in pride as he stared at this truly hellish vision in front of him.

Days later his men paraded through the streets of Denver with their "trophies." Indians heads were carried mounted on poles, while soldiers hung genitals, pubic hair and breasts from their hats and saddles.

Reaction to the news of what would become known as the "Sand Creek Massacre" was mixed across the United States. While the news of it outraged easterners, it seemed to please many people in the west. Colonel Chivington would appear before a large crowd on a Denver stage, where he regaled delighted audiences with the stories of his great "victory." He also proudly displayed 100 Indian scalps, which included the pubic "scalps" of dozens of women.

Chivington was later denounced in a congressional investigation and forced to resign. Captain Soule testified at the investigation against

---

6 Originally published in the Winter 2001 edition of *Colorado Heritage Magazine.*

Colonel Chivington and his testimony was damning. Shortly afterwards he died in a "hail" of gunfire on the streets of Denver. His murderers were never brought to justice, but the suspicion always was that he died at the orders of Colonel John Chivington.

As word of the massacre spread across the Great Plain, Indians of the southern and northern plains stiffened in their resolve to resist white encroachment. A desperate thirst for revenge swept the land, and the ramifications of that would be felt for a quarter of a century.

Over the next four years, the Plains Indians and US Army would focus their conflict on a trail used by settlers to cross the Great Plains and head either to the gold fields of modern day Montana or to continue west to California. That trail was the soon to be "infamous" Bozeman Trail.

THE BOZEMAN TRAIL

In the summer of 1863 explorers John Bozeman and John Jacobs set out to scout for a direct route from Virginia City, Montana to central Wyoming. They wanted to connect with the Oregon Trail, then the major passage used by settlers to the West Coast. Before this, most access to the southwestern Montana Territory was from St. Louis via the Missouri River to Fort Benton, Montana.

The overland Bozeman Trail followed many of the trails the Plains Indians had used since prehistoric times to travel through the Powder River Country of modern day Wyoming and Montana. This route was more direct and had more access to food and water than any previous trail used by settlers. John Bozeman, along with discovering and "blazing the trail," also made it wide enough for wagons – a crucial point for settlers. But there was a major drawback. John Bozeman's trail passed directly through territory reserved by treaty for the Sioux and Cheyenne along with Shoshone and Arapaho tribes.

Bozeman personally led the first group of about 2,000 settlers on the trail in 1864. His group and almost every subsequent group of settlers using the trail faced heavy attack by hostile Indians, furious at the encroachment of whites into their land. Washington responded by ordering the army to build a series of forts along the Bozeman trail and to protect the settlers. It wasn't long until every wagon train full of settlers that used the Bozeman Trial had a heavily armed military escort. Without that escort there was no way to successfully cross through hostile Indian territory. Even with such escorts, the loss of human life amongst the settlers using the trial was immense.

Weary of the constant attacks on settlers and the political pressure those same attacks created, President Andrew Johnson (who had replaced the recently assassinated Abraham Lincoln) ordered the army to strike back against the Sioux and Cheyenne in particular.

In response to President Johnson's orders, General John Pope assigned General Patrick Connor three columns of soldiers. These columns would invade hostile Indian territory from the Black Hills of modern-day South Dakota, to the Big Horn Mountains of modern-day Montana. General Patrick Connor was, to some Americans, a controversial choice. In 1863, Connor led an expedition against the Shoshone in Washing Territory (now modern-day Idaho and Utah). At the Battle of Bear River (many referred to it as the "Bear River Massacre"), his troops stormed the Shoshone position. Shoshone men, women, and children were slaughtered by Connor's troops, who were by all accounts completely out of control. There were numerous accounts of soldiers raping and killing women, slaughtering babies, etc.

While many Americans in the east decried the tactics used by Connor's men, General Connor defended his actions and those of his men by releasing a statement taken from one of the few Shoshone prisoners. That prisoner indicated that the warriors in the village destroyed by Connor's men had planned to attack and destroy the town of Franklin in modern-day Idaho the day after Connor's attack! If the prisoner was telling the truth, the ruthless tactics used by General Connor's troops may have saved that community.

And General Connor, with his first orders, certainly seemed to make it clear that he intended to make war on the Sioux, Arapaho, and Cheyenne in the same manner as he had done with the Shoshone. The orders he issued were blunt and to the point:

"Attack and kill every male Indian over the age of 12." [7]

---

[7] **Ibid pg 103**

Instead of Connor's troops striking the first blow, the Cheyenne and Sioux struck first. And they struck hard! On June 8, 1865, an estimated 100 Sioux and Cheyenne attacked the small, isolated, Sage Creek Station outpost, west of Fort Halleck near present-day Saratoga, Wyoming. The five soldiers and two civilians who were based in that station put up as desperate and fanatical a defense as was possible considering their small numbers. They soon ran out of ammunition, and in an act of sheer desperation they attempted to flee eight miles west to Pine Grove Station with the hostiles in hot pursuit. This was an act of almost sheer folly, as it was well known on the Plains that to flee pursuing Indians meant almost certain death. Few were fast enough to be successful. Only two of the small party from Sage Creek Station escaped to the safety of Pine Grove Station. The Sioux, Cheyenne, and Arapaho continued their raids, focusing mainly on stage coaches and hit and run attacks on army patrols. On June 9th they killed 11 soldiers in a well-executed ambush near Fort Benton on the Missouri River.

By July 1865, over 10,000 Cheyenne and Sioux were camped along the Power River near modern day Cheyenne, Wyoming. Remembering the slaughter of their people at Sand Creek, the Indians decided it was time to attack the soldiers at Platte Bridge Station, an army post near present-day Casper, Wyoming.

Platte Bridge Station was built in 1862 at the site of a trading post. It served to house the batteries and other supplies for the Pacific Telegraph line. The duties of the soldiers stationed there included protecting and repairing the telegraph line along with nearby white settlers. Their duties had gotten more challenging after the Sand Creek bloodshed as Plains Indians, in a fury over the massacre of the Cheyenne there had, amongst others things, destroyed miles of telegraph wires and their supporting infrastructure. This was an isolated post on its own, a perfect target for "whipped up" warriors to attack.

In July 1865, over a thousand hostile Sioux and Cheyenne warriors moved towards the small army post. On July 21, 1865, a detachment led by Commissary Sergeant Amos Custard left Platte Bridge Station with their destination being the US Army post at Sweetwater Station 55 miles away. After delivering rations and other supplies to the post at Sweetwater Station, Sergeant Custard and his detachment began the return trip to Platte Bridge Station. On July 26th they quickly became surrounded by a large group of hostile warriors near what was known as Red Buttes, within sight of the post at Platte Bridge Station. Lieutenant Caspar Collins led a group of 20 troopers out of Platte Bridge Station in an effort to relieve Custard's wagon train. Collins men were ambushed and, in a short furious firefight, Collins and many of his men were killed. Lieutenant Collins died very bravely while covering the retreat of his men. Reports indicated he had been badly wounded, and yet he ordered his men to escape and covered their retreat while blazing away with his handgun until he was killed. The modern-day city of Casper, Wyoming, although spelled differently, is named in his honor.

By now, Custard and his wagon train were totally surrounded. He was within sight of Platte Bridge Station but he was to get no further. After defeating Lieutenant Collins' small party, over 1,000 Sioux and Cheyenne launched a savage attack on Sergeant Custard's wagon train. Custard, thinking quickly, ordered his wagons into a circle to use as barricades and fought desperately against overwhelming numbers of warriors. His twenty men, sheltering from behind the wagons, pumped volley after volley from their Spencer repeating rifles into the swarming hostiles. As the screaming Sioux and Cheyenne first charged them and then rode in circles around them firing rifles and arrows into them, the soldiers, firing their now red-hot rifles, repulsed them, inflicting dozens of casualties. When the Indians briefly retreated, the soldiers frantically built barricades of bedding, bales of cotton and boxes. Most of the troopers fired from under the wagons, as that provided them good cover. However, a small group of men inside one wagon took a deadly toll of hostiles by firing through slits cut in the canvas cover. Sergeant Amos Custard ran from wagon to wagon, keeping up the fighting spirits of his men and urging them to hold on until more help came from Platte Bridget Station. They could see the post and they knew help would be coming!

Despite all their brave, dogged resistance, the Indians still surrounded them. And no help came from the Platte Bridge Station post. The commanding officers at the post, looking out, realized that no relief party could possibly cut its way through to the wagon train. Lieutenant Collins had tried and had met with disaster. Sergeant Custard was on his own.

For over four hours, Custard's men fought on, doing all they could to hold off the enemy. A horrified Sergeant Pennock, based in the post at Platte Bridge Station, later wrote in his diary: 'All this we could plainly see from the station, but we could do nothing for them....We could see the Indians in swarms charge down on our boys when they would roll volley after volley into them.'

One can only imagine the horror Sergeant Pennock and the other troopers inside Platte Bridge Station felt, watching their comrades – in easy eyesight of them - facing certain death while they could do nothing to help them.

The end would soon come to Sergeant Custard and his gallant men. Realizing that charging headlong into the troopers' heavy fire was foolhardy, the hostiles began to dig trenches with knives and tomahawks; they carried logs and rocks over to roll forward as a movable breastwork and fired their guns and arrows into the wagons. They moved closer and closer despite the furious fire from the soldiers. At about 4 p.m., the end came. After firing a volley, into Custard's position the hostiles charged into the wagons. Savage hand to hand combat broke out. Soldiers swung rifles as clubs, fired handguns, and buried razor sharp knives into their foes while the hostiles swung spiked war clubs, and tomahawks. Skulls were crushed, throats slashed, chests and abdomens torn open by knives. No mercy was given, nor expected, by either side. The end result was inevitable. The yelling and firing ended and the wagons began burning. The hostiles moved off with what they had looted from the wagons and with the scalps of the dead soldiers. There were no survivors from Sergeant Amos Custard's valiant command.

Things were not going much better for General Connor's columns. One column commanded by Colonel Nelson Cole marched about 560 miles from Omaha, Nebraska, to modern-day Sturgis, South Dakota, without encountering a single hostile Indian. By the time they reached Sturgis, his men were suffering from lack of water and food, and wagons that were falling apart from the strain of the long march. At Sturgis, Cole's command linked up with a column commanded by Colonel Samuel Walker. Walker, like Cole, had encountered no Indians, and his men were also suffering from lack of supplies. The two officers decided to march towards the Powder River country of Wyoming. They would march separately but close enough that they could coordinate their actions in time of battle. Once they reached the Powder River territory they hoped to join forces with General Connor, who was thought to be in that area.

By the time Cole's and Walker's troops reached the Powder River area, most of the soldiers were barefoot, their boots having fallen apart. Horses and mules were dying, and the men were suffering greatly from lack of water and food. On September 1st, near Broadus, Montana, the two columns finally made contact with the hostiles. About 300 Sioux raided the soldiers' horse herd in a surprise ambush. Unlike the troops of Lieutenant Caspar Collins and Sergeant Amos Custard, the soldiers guarding the horses didn't put up a brave fight. They simply "dropped their guns and ran." Six soldiers were killed. It was a simply dreadful performance by the military.

Colonels Cole and Walker then pushed on north to the mouth of the

Mizpah River east of Miles City, Montana. Completely frustrated by this time, and almost out of supplies, Colonels Cole and Walker decided to retrace their steps south along the Powder River to look for General Connor. They were attacked again on September 5th near Powderville, Montana by 1,000 Cheyenne and Sioux. Walker and Cole's men put up a furious resistance this time and beat off the Indian attack.

On September 8 and 9 the two columns were again attacked and once again were forced to fight desperately for their very survival. By this time both Colonels Walker and Cole could admit they were whipped. Their battered commands staggered into Fort Connor (later renamed Fort Reno) on September 20th. General Connor was awaiting them there. The soldiers under Cole and Walker had stretched their 60 days of rations to over 80 days. They were half starved, and there was a trail of dead horses and mules littering their path to the fort. Connor was so appalled by the poor condition of Cole and Walker's commands that he deemed them unfit for further service and sent them to Fort Laramie, where most of them were subsequently mustered out of military service.

General Connor himself had mild success in his expedition. On August 29th his column discovered and destroyed a large Arapaho village located on the Tongue River. When Connor retreated from the burning village, his column was harassed day and night by enraged Arapaho warriors (many of whom had not been present during the battle). Connor's forces killed 63 Arapaho while suffering only eight dead of their own. It was the only success Connor could point to during this long expedition. And it wasn't a true "success" as previous to his attack, the Arapaho, while not being overly friendly to whites, were also not overly hostile. Connor's attack pushed the Arapaho firmly into the hostile camp.

General Pope wasn't pleased with the outcome of Connor's expedition. The press across the United States referred to Connor's expedition as "'" a dismal failure" carried out with "large, ungainly columns filled with troops anxious to get home now that the Civil War was over." [8] General Pope abolished the District of the Plains (which he had just established earlier in the summer) and relieved Connor of his command, reassigning him back to duty in Utah.

General Pope now resolved to try a new tactic to protect the settlers using the Bozeman Trial. On March 10, 1866, Pope issued General Order 33. This order, among other things, created the new Mountain District, which would encompass the vast territory stretching from the North Platte to Virginia City. It also authorized the building of three new forts to protect the Bozeman Trial settlers. One of those forts, Fort Phil Kearny, and its commanding officer Colonel Henry Carrington, would forever be burned into the memories of soldiers, Indians, and the American public.

---

8 Major General Patrick Edward Connor" The California Military Museum
http://www.military.museum.org/Conner.html

Colonel Henry B. Carrington

Margaret Carrington

COLONEL HENRY CARRINGTON

Henry Beebee Carrington was born on March 2, 1824, in Wallingford, Connecticut. He was raised by his mother and grandmother. They were strong abolitionists, and quickly indoctrinated the young Henry with evangelical and anti-slavery beliefs. These beliefs were strongly reinforced when, as a young man attending school in Torringford, Connecticut, he attended a speech by the fiery abolitionist John Brown. Carrington was mesmerized by the charismatic Brown, and firmly agreed with his anti-slavery views. Later he witnessed riots and other civil disorder directed against abolitionists. These experiences placed Carrington even more firmly into the abolitionist camp.

Upon finishing his schooling, Carrington, who had a strong interest in the military, applied for admission to the United States Military Academy (West Point). Although he was intellectually brilliant, and more than capable of passing the academic entrance exams, Carrington failed the physical exams. This was due to recurring lung issues resulting from the fact that he was a carrier of tuberculosis his entire adult life. (Later he would suffer the agony of seeing both his wives and a number of his children die from this terrible disease.) As a result of being denied entrance into West Point, Carrington instead applied and was accepted into Yale University in 1841.

Carrington graduated from Yale in 1845. For the next two years, he taught Natural Science and Greek at the Irving Institute in Tarrytown, New York. Carrington, a brilliant academic man, then decided to continue his education. He returned to Yale in 1847 to study law. He graduated, taught briefly at a women's college, and in 1848 moved west to Columbus, Ohio to join his cousin's law practice. Over the next number of years, Carrington developed a reputation as a gifted, hard-working lawyer and a devout church-going Christian. In 1851, he married a young woman named Margaret Sullivant, who was part of a wealthy, very influential Columbus family.

In 1854, Carrington - who was already well established due to his hard work as a lawyer and his marriage to Margaret Sullivant - then made a connection that would change his life. At an abolitionist conference, he met Ohio Senator Salmon Chase. Chase was a fierce abolitionist who regularly used his political connections to help fellow abolitionists to get ahead. That year, Carrington helped organize the Ohio Republican Party, and in 1855, when Chase was elected Governor of Ohio, Carrington assisted him with his campaign. In his second term in office, Chase appointed Carrington as Adjutant General of Ohio. This role placed Carrington in command of the Ohio State Militia. It was the perfect role for the young and upcoming Carrington. He still had military ambitions, and this office would allow him a military role, while his legal work showed him to be a disciplined, superbly organized and tireless worker. As Governor Chase had publicly declared that a strong priority of his administration was to reorganize the state militia, he could not have picked a more able man to handle this task than Carrington.

Despite Carrington's superb work after he took over this role, his office was still swamped by recruits when war broke out between the North and the Southern states in 1861. Thousands of young Ohio men descended on recruiting offices as President Lincoln had issued a call for 75,000 state militiamen to report for duty to protect the Union against the Southern rebels. Even Carrington, a man gifted with outstanding administrative skills, was almost overwhelmed by the enormous task of recruiting, clothing, and feeding thousands of recruits in a short period of time. Some newspapers printed articles critical of Carrington's early performance but within a month

Carrington was able to report (honestly) that he had filled Ohio's quota of 10,000 recruits and that he could even provide up to eight additional regiments of troops if needed.

Carrington was later given credit for devising plans to use these additional regiments to protect the areas of Ohio bordering on the mountain regions of West Virginia and various railway terminals on both sides of the Ohio River. This indicated that not only did he have a true talent for planning and administration – he also had a "good eye" for defensive planning and fortifications.

In June 1861, Salmon Chase, now President Lincoln's Secretary of the Treasury, arranged for Carrington to receive a commission as Colonel of the newly created 18th Infantry Regiment. Carrington did express some concern that other, more experienced officers already in service would resent him receiving a commission as a Colonel. Chase however assured him that anybody who had seen the superb work he had done with the militia in Ohio would respect his new commission. That being said, Chase was well aware that Carrington had a gift for administration and planning. He wasn't so sure that Carrington had a knack for combat, and as a result he told Carrington that he didn't feel he (Carrington) would actually be sent into battle.

(Carrington also lacked the "look" of a combat officer. He was short and of slight build. He had a dark beard, and he wore his hair long. His eyes were described as "sensitive," and they sat deep under a high forehead. He looked more like a university professor – which he had been – than a military officer.)

Chase's assumption was proven to be correct. Carrington spent the rest of the war in Indiana and Ohio, recruiting and training the men who would make up the 18th Infantry Regiment and help it to establish itself as one of the Union Army's most decorated regiments of the war. Carrington never did see any combat in the war.

One event that would prove to be eventually life-changing for Carrington occurred in the summer of 1861, after he had taken command of the 18th Infantry Regiment. He had established the headquarters for his regiment in Columbus, Ohio. In early August 1861, he built Camp Thomas, located four miles north of Columbus. This camp would be the base where Ohio volunteers would be trained for combat duty. One of the first men to report for duty at Camp Thomas to assist Carrington was Lieutenant William Judd Fetterman.

Captain William J. Fetterman

CAPTAIN WILLIAM J. FETTERMAN

William Judd Fetterman was born in 1833. The exact day and month of his birth has been lost to history. It is thought that he was born in New London, Connecticut, but that too is not known for sure. From his earliest days, young William had a strong interest in the military. This was driven by his father, who was a graduate of West Point, and an uncle who assisted him when his father died in 1842. William's uncle had served with great distinction in the war with Mexico.

In 1853, Fetterman applied to and was rejected by West Point. He then turned to a business career in banking. However, his heart was still set on a military career. This came to fruition in 1861 with the outbreak of the Civil War. On May 14th of that year, Fetterman enlisted in the Union Army. Due to his social graces, learned through his banking career, Fetterman was almost immediately commissioned as a First Lieutenant and was assigned to Camp Thomas, where he would serve under Colonel Carrington.

Fetterman made an outstanding first impression upon Carrington. He was a hard worker, ambitious, talented, and well-organized (much like Carrington was), while Margaret Carrington described him as *"commanding esteem by his refinement, gentlemanly manners, and adaption to social life."*[9]

By all contemporary accounts, Carrington and Fetterman worked very well together as they turned the brand new 18th Infantry Regiment into a disciplined, well-trained fighting force. Fetterman also established a reputation at this time as being a superb recruiter,

---

[9] Smith, Shannon, *Give Me Eighty Men, Women and the Myth of the Fetterman Fight*, Lincoln, University of Nebraska Press, 2008, page 19.

ably filling the ranks of the 18th Infantry with top quality recruits.

In November 1861, Carrington assigned command of Company A of the 18th Infantry Regiment's Second Battalion to First Lieutenant Fetterman. Fetterman and his company then moved out to the front. He participated in the siege of Corinth, Mississippi, in April and May of 1862.

On December 31, 1862, Fetterman and his command, under the leadership of Union General William Rosecrans, clashed with Confederate forces commanded by General Braxton Braggs at what would become known as the Battle of Stones River, just outside of Murfreesboro, Tennessee. This would become one of the bloodiest and most ferociously fought battles of the Civil War. Out of a total of approximately 81,000 soldiers on both sides, over 24,000 became casualties - a casualty rate second only to the Battle of Gettysburg. After five days of non-stop bloody fighting, the Confederate forces finally withdrew.

Fetterman's performance in this savage bloodbath was simply outstanding. Even though the 18th Infantry lost almost half its men in a single hour of fighting, Fetterman provided superb leadership. He personally fought ferociously and used superb military judgment in deploying his men. Fetterman was not an officer who stayed in the rear and directed his troops. He fought right alongside them, and for this trait he quickly established himself as a "fighting man's officer". His troops thus awarded him deep respect.

That respect was also shown to Fetterman by his colleagues, and was reflected in numerous dispatches and reports: "Captain Fetterman's command marched to my assistance with great promptness...conspicuous for gallantry and bravery...displayed great gallantry and spirit...the conduct of Captain Fetterman in throwing up a salient and maintaining his positions against repeated attempts to dislodge him by the enemy, is worthy of particular notice..."[10]

The performance of the 18th Infantry at Stones River established that regiment with a well-deserved reputation of a highly disciplined, tough fighting unit. Fetterman as a result was given a brevet promotion to major.

In April 1863, Fetterman was reassigned to recruitment duties in Pittsburgh. He had shown in the past that he was an excellent recruiter, and the US Army didn't forget that. With the Confederates now driving into Pennsylvania, Northern morale was dropping and fewer young men were joining the Union forces. Fetterman was determined to turn that around.

One year later, after successful recruitment duties, Fetterman requested to rejoin his command. His request was granted and, after a superb combat performance in Georgia, Fetterman was given command of the entire Second Battalion of the 18th Infantry. The Second Battalion was made up of eight companies of approximately 100 soldiers per company. His forces were part of General Sherman's march on Atlanta. Fetterman's performance was so outstanding that he was then named Acting Assistant Adjutant General of the Fourteenth Corps, to which his own regiment belonged. This exposed him to the very highest levels of military communication flowing from the battlefield to and from Washington. William J. Fetterman was very clearly a "rising star" in the officer ranks of the US Army. At the same time he still retained command of the Second Battalion of the 18th Infantry. Fetterman, still leading his troops "from the front," personally led them into several battles around Atlanta. This led him to receive another brevet promotion – this time to that of Lieutenant Colonel.

---

10 US War Dept., *The War of the Rebellion...Official Records,* Ser I, Vol 38, Pt I, 94,527,558,560,577-8,586-8.

Fetterman retained command of the Second Battalion and served as Acting Assistant Adjutant General of the Fourteenth Corp for the remainder of the war. By the end of the war, Fetterman had firmly established himself as an outstanding combat officer, as well as a very able and experienced administrative officer. He felt his future within the military was very bright. Unlike many of his colleagues, who left military service at the end of the war, William Fetterman decided to remain in the army.

In June 1865, Fetterman briefly rejoined Colonel Carrington at Camp Thomas. There the two officers began planning the reorganization of the 18th Infantry at war's end. Fetterman was not there long as in the fall of 1865 he was assigned to recruitment duties in Cleveland. Carrington meanwhile was ordered to join the 18th Infantry Regiment in Louisville, Kentucky. Shortly after arriving in Louisville, Carrington and the 18th received orders to proceed to Fort Kearny, Nebraska Territory. Carrington and his regiment were moving west and with that would enter history.

THE JOURNEY WEST

On November 5, 1865 Colonel Carrington and his family along with the 18th Infantry Regiment headed west via trains and Missouri River steamships to Fort Leavenworth, Kansas. After a short stay there, they began a 16-day march to Fort Kearny, Nebraska. It was a brutal experience for Carrington's family and his troops. Temperatures dropped well below zero, and in her diary Margaret Carrington described how up to two feet of snow would have to be cleared before tents could be pitched. After two brutally hard weeks of marching through subzero temperatures and deep snow, the 18th staggered through the gates of Fort Kearny, Nebraska, on December 11, 1865.

Carrington and the 18th "hunkered down" at Fort Kearny for the next four plus months. The time was spent recruiting and drilling troops while they awaited new orders.

Those orders arrived on March 10, 1866, when General John Pope issued General Order Number 33. Among others things, this order created the Mountain District to protect the Bozeman Trail and assigned the commanding officer of the 18th Infantry Regiment (Colonel Carrington) to take command of the Mountain District. The same day this order was issued, Generals Ulysses S. Grant and William Sherman were debating further changes in the army. Grant had decided to create the Department of the Platte and assign 56-year-old General Philip St. George Cooke to command it. The Mountain District would be part of the Department of the Platte. Sherman implored upon Grant not to assign this duty to Cooke. He stated: "We need a young General, who can travel and see with his own eyes and if need be command both whites and Indians to keep the Peace." [11]

Despite the best efforts of Sherman, Grant insisted on appointing Cooke. "On the surface," it didn't appear to be a poor choice. Cooke was born in 1809 and graduated from West Point in 1827. He served with distinction in the Black Hawk War and the War with Mexico. In 1858, Cooke wrote a two-volume manual on cavalry tactics that was adopted and put to extensive use during the Civil War. During the war itself, Cooke saw extensive action in the defense of Washington and such battles as Williamsburg, Gaines' Mill and White Oak Swamp. He blundered terribly during the Gaines' Mill battle when he unwisely ordered the 5th US Cavalry to charge a heavily-defended Confederate position, resulting in the almost total destruction of that regiment. Cooke also suffered severe embarrassment due to the fact that his son-in-law J.E.B. Stuart was a brilliant cavalry commander in the Confederate Army whose actions usually resulted in an embarrassing defeat for his Union opponents. Still, even with these errors and embarrassment, Cooke was a well-respected senior officer.

Cooke found out about his new posting while reading the newspaper in New York City. Grant had not spoken to him about this assignment, so to say that he was surprised would be an understatement. He was unaware that Colonel Carrington would report to him until he reported for duty to General Sherman in St. Louis five weeks later. He and Carrington had never met, and by the time Cooke was aware that Carrington was his subordinate, Carrington was already preparing to continue his journey west from Fort Kearny.

In fact, Colonel Carrington would report to General Cooke for approximately nine months. In that time they would never meet.

---

11 Carrington, Margaret *Absaraka, Home of the Crows,* Chicago,: R.R. Donnelley and Sons, 1950, pg 13.

Cooke set up his headquarters in Omaha, Nebraska, and he and Carrington would communicate over a distance of close to 800 miles through telegraphs and mounted couriers. It would be essentially impossible for Cooke to have a clear idea of the challenges Carrington would face on a daily basis.

On March 28, 1866, Colonel Carrington received orders "to move immediately" to occupy Fort Reno in Dakota Territory (in modern day Johnson County, Wyoming), and from there to build two forts along the Bozeman Trail. He was promised all the supplies that he would require - even a water-powered saw mill! Carrington was pleased with these promises. However, he was concerned that at the present time he only had 220 soldiers – about a quarter of the battalion's authorized strength - and his troops were armed with obsolete muzzle-loading Springfield muskets. This was not a force that was going to strike fear into the hostile Plains Indians! Carrington immediately asked his superiors where his promised recruits were (few had shown up) and requested a departure delay in order to better prepare his troops and await further reinforcements.

On April 13, 1866, he received his first formal orders from General Cooke emphasizing that he (Carrington) was in charge of the Mountain District. Carrington recorded: 'Immediately on receipt of the order establishing the Mountain District, I issued General Order No 1, assuming command, and made requisition for the commissary and quartermaster supplies for one year, upon the full basis of eight hundred men, and fifty per cent additional for wastage and contingencies." [12]

It is interesting to note that Carrington only had 220 troops under his command, yet he was ordering supplies for a force of 800. Clearly he was "holding out" for a much larger force before he marched into

---

12 US Congress, 50th, 1st sess. Senate executive document 33,2.

hostile territory. Carrington, in fact, waited at Fort Kearny until April 26, when he received further orders from General Cooke. Cooke was livid that Carrington had not acted on the orders of March 28 to "move immediately," and he sanctioned Carrington for this failure to act.

Carrington responded in his own defense with a long letter outlining all the steps he had taken to prepare his force for marching. He described how he had assembled 50 wagon teams and loaded them with tools and supplies to build forts, obtained 200 horses, and gathered instruments for measuring distances and surveying routes. He also obtained over 200 seven-shot Spencer Carbines. These weapons were a vast improvement over the single-shot Springfield muskets that his troops still carried. (Carrington, however, issued the Spencer carbines to members of the regimental band and left his infantry still equipped with the obsolete Springfields. He had decided to train some of his infantry on horsemanship skills with some of the 200 horses he had obtained. His infantrymen, however, were struggling to learn how to ride properly and handle the long Springfield muskets while on horseback.) Finally, Carrington went into great detail regarding the amount of food and seeds he had gathered. All this was quickly sent off to Cooke in a dispatch.

As Carrington waited for additional orders from Cooke, he and his officers began thinking seriously about the territory they would be marching into. To say there was deep concern would be a vast understatement. There were no official guidebooks available. Maps showed little. They read the reports from explorers Lewis and Clark who had surveyed the area from 1804-1806. With such little information the officers were not sure what the territory even looked like. Was it mountainous or flat? Was it barren or was it covered in vegetation? Really all they knew for sure was that the Sioux and Cheyenne Indians viewed this area as very precious to them, and that the US government viewed it as the most direct emigration route to Montana.

On May 13, 1866, the 3rd Battalion of the 18th Infantry marched into Fort Kearny from Fort Leavenworth. They added several hundred new troops to the force that Carrington would take out west. There was a touch of "comedy of errors" when the latest troops arrived. The 3rd Battalion had marched out of Fort Leavenworth assuming the 2nd Battalion had plentiful stocks of rations in Fort Kearny. That wasn't the case at all, and Carrington had assumed that the 3rd Battalion was bringing with them badly needed supplies. The result was a large number of hungry soldiers who were now awaiting an overdue wagon train with rations and other supplies.

On May 16th, the long awaited wagon train arrived. With the wagon train was a surprise visitor – Lieutenant General William T. Sherman. Sherman, one of the Union's greatest Civil War heroes, was in fine spirits when he visited Carrington's command at Fort Kearny. Margaret Carrington wrote in her diary that "Sherman entered into the plans for the expedition with his usual energy and skill." [13]

Sherman had little experience in any manner with the Plains Indians, and thus he encouraged the women and children at Fort Kearny to accompany their spouses/fathers on the upcoming expedition. He also encouraged the women to keep diaries so that their experiences would be recorded for history. Like most contemporary military officers, Sherman had total confidence in the ability of the US Army to defeat any force of hostiles that they would encounter.

After a short visit, Sherman departed. Then on May 19, 1866, Carrington's column left Fort Kearny. It was a massive expedition. There were more than 1,000 men – over 700 soldiers and 300 civilians - along with 226 wagons loaded with supplies. The supplies included everything that would be needed to construct and supply

---

13 Brown, Dee, *The Fetterman Massacre* London, Pan Books, Ltd., 1974 pg 27.

three new forts. They included building tools, windows, two sawmills, and equipment to mow grass and build roofing shingles. Carrington's beloved regimental band had their brass instruments packed and all the officers' household goods – chairs, beds, cutlery, dishes, etc., were packed along with ammunition and weapons. (Carrington, however, was concerned – his ammunition stocks were less than plentiful. He did not feel that he had anywhere near enough ammunition to fight a prolonged campaign. These concerns were strongly communicated to General Cooke in numerous dispatches.) There were also oxen, horses, mules, chickens, pigs, and turkeys accompanying the column. One witness referred to the massive expedition as *"Carrington's Overland Circus."* [14]

As Carrington's column slowly worked its way west, he began to turn to his scouts, in particular the legendary western "mountain man" Jim Bridger for advice and guidance.

Jim Bridger was born in 1804 and, as a young man in 1822, began a long career as a "mountain man" guide and scout. He was fluent in English, French, Spanish, and several Plains Indian dialects. He explored the Rocky Mountains and Great Plains from the United States and well into what would become Canada. In 1850, he discovered what would become known as "Bridger's Pass," which shortened the Oregon Trail by over 60 miles and, in the 20th Century, would become part of Interstate 80. In 1864, he blazed the "Bridger Trail" which was an alternative route from modern-day Wyoming to the gold fields of what would become Montana. This new route avoided the ever dangerous Bozeman Trail which Carrington and his force had set out to guard. In 1866, the army hired Bridger to accompany Carrington as an advisor and guide.

On May 30th, the First Battalion – almost half of Carrington's force –

---

[14] Smith, Shannon, *Give Me Eighty Men,* pg 27.

split off from Carrington and proceeded to duty stations in Colorado, Utah, and Kansas. On June 13, Carrington and the Second Battalion reached Fort Laramie. Their timing could not have been worse. Spotted Tail, the most influential of the Brule Sioux, had been convinced to come to Fort Laramie to meet with Commissioners of the US Government to discuss access through Sioux territory (i.e.; the Bozeman Trail) for white emigrants, miners, and the military. The Oglala Sioux led by Red Cloud arrived with the Brule to join the talks. To try to convince the Sioux to allow this access, the government gave Spotted Tail and all his other various chiefs and people presents consisting of clothing, old military uniforms (warriors liked wearing military hats, trousers and jackets) and tools, as well as money.

As the talks were ongoing, Carrington and the First Battalion of the 18th Infantry Regiment marched into Fort Laramie. The Sioux were beyond outraged by this. In their minds, they were at the talks as equals and had not agreed to anything yet. Then, during the talks troops arrive. Were the troops there to intimidate them? Or to take over the Bozeman Trail whether the Sioux agreed to terms or not? One Sioux chief commented: "Great Father send us presents and wants new road, but white chief goes with soldiers to steal road before Indian say yes or no."

The Oglala, led by Red Cloud and Man-Afraid-Of-His-Horses, stormed out of the talks. Those who remained agreed to allow the Bozeman Trail to be used by whites and for the military to build forts along it. The Oglala, however, vowed to stop all white incursions into their territory. Red Cloud in particular was so infuriated that he went so far as to visit the traditional enemy of the Sioux, the Crow nation, and he asked the Crows to join the Sioux in an alliance against the whites. The Crow, however, declined as they still hoped to find some form of accommodation with the whites.

After four days of rest at Fort Laramie, Carrington and his force resumed their march north on the Bozeman Trail, heading directly into the territory that Red Cloud and his supporters were prepared to defend to the death. Their destination would be Fort Connor (named after General Patrick Connor), 150 miles north of Fort Laramie in central modern-day Wyoming.

Red Cloud was unsuccessful in convincing the Crow to join him in a war with the United States. However, he was successful in convincing an immense number of fellow Sioux to join with him. By late summer, his camp consisted of over 500 lodges, representing over 2,000 warriors and their families. His camp lay along the Tongue River right in the heart of Carrington's Mountain District. There was plenty of water and grass to support the camp's inhabitants. It was also a prime hunting area. Red Cloud would be able to stay there for an indefinite period of time. Meanwhile as author Shannon Smith described in her book "Give Me Eighty Good Men...." "Meanwhile, Carrington and his entourage, 'splendidly furnished with everything except arms, ammunition, and horses' as an early writer of the event aptly stated, continued his march directly towards them." [15]

After two weeks of hard marching, Carrington and his column reached Fort Connor. During the march, Carrington wisely listened to Jim Bridger, who urged him to send out advance scouts and increase security on the flanks of the column. Bridger knew they were moving into the heart of Sioux territory, and that the Sioux were in an "ugly mood." Fort Connor was manned by two companies of "Galvanized Yankees" - former Confederate soldiers who had gained their release from prisoner of war camps by agreeing to serve on the Western Frontier and fight Indians. Carrington moved quickly to release the former Confederates from service. He relocated Fort Connor several miles north and renamed it Fort Reno. With Fort Reno thus established, Carrington assigned two companies of the

---

15 Ibid, pg 30.

Second Battalion to garrison the fort, and then continued west with now fewer than 400 men under arms.

On July 15, 1866, Carrington's column reached the site of what would become Fort Philip Kearny. (Philip Kearny was a popular, one-armed Union general, killed in action in 1862 during the Civil War. The formal name of the fort would be Fort Philip Kearny however it was almost always referred to as Fort Phil Kearny.) Carrington surveyed the area and turned to his wife Margaret and declared, "Margaret this is the location! It is perfect. There is plenty of forage for the livestock, and water. We have a good supply of wood for construction and by placing the fort right here, our sentries can see anyone approaching us for miles."

"I can see that Henry", Margaret Carrington responded. "It is a splendid choice for the location of our new home!"

Fort Phil Kearny was to be built on an elevated plateau situated between forks of Piney Creek. The area had extensive grass (very important to feed the livestock) and a good natural water supply. Outside of the grass and water, this location offered a perfect 360 degree view of the surrounding area. Once the stockade walls were built, nobody could approach the fort without being spotted by the sentries. The one downside to the location was that the fort required wood for building supplies and for heating and cooking fires. The closest wood was in a "pinery" (as the wooded areas were referred to) located five miles to the west of the fort. This meant that parties of men who were sent to cut wood that the fort badly required would be exposed to attack by Sioux and Cheyenne warriors on a regular basis. The threat of attack would necessitate the wood-cutting parties being escorted by soldiers both to and from the pinery and while they were cutting wood.

Fort Phil Kearny was to be a 400-foot square, with 1600 feet of wooden stockade enclosing barracks, officers' quarters, administrative offices and buildings, a sutler's store,[16] warehouses, hospital, and ammunition magazine, among others. In the southeast portion of the main fort was to be a quartermaster's yard of approximately 200X600 feet. This would contain stables, mechanics sheds, quarters for the civilian teamsters, a wood yard and a hay yard. The log stockade enclosing the fort would be about eight feet high, with a continuous platform (better known as a banquette) encircling it that soldiers could kneel or stand on. There were to be flaring loopholes at every fourth log that soldiers could fire out of at approaching hostiles.

On July 16th, a party of Cheyenne approached the site of the new fort. Carrington had been warned two days earlier, by a civilian interpreter assigned to him by the name of Jack Stead, that these Cheyenne were approaching but were willing to talk peace with Carrington. The Cheyenne numbering about 40 in total appeared, just as Stead had predicted, waving white flags. Carrington and his officers greeted them wearing their dress uniforms in an effort to impress the Cheyenne. Once all were seated in the large hospital tent that Carrington had ordered erected, he then, in a further effort to impress the Indians with his military strength, ordered one of the regiments' howitzers to be fired. The Cheyenne were duly impressed when the shell fired from the weapon exploded in the distant hills.

After that impressive display, talks began. Cheyenne chief Black Horse, speaking through Jack Stead, informed Carrington that he, along with 176 Cheyenne lodges, had broken away from a much larger force of Cheyenne. Black Horse and those with him wished peace. The other Cheyenne were joining with Red Cloud and the Sioux in an effort to drive all whites from the Powder River country.

---

16 The sutler was a civilian merchant who sold various goods to army personnel. He usually had a stores within a fort and at times would accompany the army into the field and operate from a wagon.

He also informed Carrington that his force had been under daily surveillance since leaving Fort Reno. Red Cloud knew exactly where he was and how big a force Carrington commanded. Finally, Black Horse warned Carrington that Red Cloud's warriors had positioned themselves towards the Powder River cutting off all further approaches to Carrington's position. The only way additional supplies and/or troops could reach Carrington was to fight their way through. Later that evening, Black Horse and the other Cheyenne departed. Carrington and his forces were now alone, deep in the heart of Sioux and Cheyenne territory.

From "day one" it became evident that there was not a "threat" of attack. Attacks were in fact a reality. They began immediately. At 5 am on July 17th, Sioux warriors infiltrated through the sentries and stampeded a large force of horses and other livestock. Captain Henry Hammond led a mounted column out in pursuit. Carrington then ordered the camp prepared to defend itself. He had the howitzers loaded and prepared to fire, and deployed other troops into defensive positions. He sent Lieutenant William Bisbee with 50 mounted soldiers and two companies of infantry to support Captain Hammond. Bisbee encountered Hammond retreating. Hammond had recovered four of the animals. However, he had been attacked, and suffered two dead and three wounded. It was a terrible exchange – five killed or wounded soldiers in exchange for recovering four animals.

As the combined force returned to Carrington's camp, they came across a horrific scene. They encountered the wagons of a trader known as "French Pete" Gazzous. The wagons were destroyed and the bodies of Gazzous and five others lay in the camp. The bodies were mutilated and bristling with arrows. What was so shocking was Gazzous was married to a Sioux woman and was known to have cordial relations with Red Cloud and the other Sioux. He and his camp had been massacred by his wife's own people. It was becoming more apparent to all that Red Cloud's fury towards whites knew no boundaries.

On July 20th, Red Cloud's warriors attacked a wagon train near Crazy Woman Creek, along the Powder River, that was destined to join Carrington. As the wagon train approached Crazy Woman Creek, off in the distance near a grove of cotton woods were numerous dark moving objects. Lieutenant Nathaniel Daniels peered through his field glasses and informed Lieutenant George Templeton that the objects appeared to be a small herd of buffalo. Templeton suggested the buffalo be hunted. Fresh buffalo meat would be welcomed by all in the wagon train. The two officers rode ahead to try to turn the herd towards the wagon train. The men in the wagons grabbed rifles, and the wagon train steered towards the herd of buffalo.

As the wagons moved through a dry creek, the air suddenly exploded in a hail of incoming arrows and bullets. War whoops from seemingly hundreds of Sioux warriors pierced the air. It was a miracle that there were no casualties from this first attack. With the men armed to hunt buffalo, they were in a position to return fire quickly, which was exactly what they did. This quick reaction may have saved the wagon train. Lieutenant James Bradley ordered the wagons "corralled" (organized into a circular pattern.) Then he led a squad of a dozen troops charging up a slope, driving the Sioux back. Moments later, a rider less army mount came galloping into the corralled wagons. It was Lieutenant Daniel's mount, and there were numerous arrows protruding from the poor beast. Templeton then galloped in, his horse bristling with arrows and he himself with an arrow buried in his back. The surgeon assigned to the wagon train was able to remove the arrow from Templeton, but was unable to further treat his wounds as the Sioux resumed their attacks and he was needed to assist in the defense. Templeton lay in agony while several women did their best to comfort him.

The wagon train had an escort of 37 soldiers. These soldiers were quickly fighting for their own lives as well as trying to defend the civilians in the wagon train. The wagons were circled and for hours a raging battle occurred. Approximately 160 Sioux poured rifle and arrow fire into the wagon trains. At one point, Lieutenant Alexander Wands, who due to his vast Civil War experience, had assumed command with Templeton wounded and out of action, realized that their current position could not be held. Half a mile to the south was a small, treeless hill. If they could somehow advance to that hill, it would be a far superior defensive position from which to try to hold the Sioux off. Wands ordered the wagons grouped together, two in the front, the ambulances with the wounded and woman and children following, and three wagons in the rear. Wands, along with Lieutenant Prescott Skinner and 12 troopers, would cover the flanks and lead the advance while Lieutenant Bradley, with seven troopers would serve as the rear guard.

Knowing that to be cautious was to invite disaster, Wands and Skinner led a furious cavalry charge up the hill and drove the Sioux from the position. Lieutenant Bradley's rear guard fought furiously to keep the Sioux at bay, and in quick fashion the wagons reached the pinnacle of the hill and were corralled into defensive formations.

Recovering from their initial surprise, the Sioux quickly resumed their attack. The civilians, including women and children, sought cover wherever they could find it, while the soldiers and male civilians returned fire. Casualties were mounting among the whites and ammunition was running low. A council was held between the officers and male civilians. It was finally agreed that if all looked to be lost, the wounded would be mercifully killed and then the soldiers would kill the women and children before killing themselves. At all costs nobody could be allowed to fall into the hands of the hostiles to face a horrific death of slow torture and, in the case of women, certain rape. Chaplain David White, one of the civilians traveling with the wagon train, could not agree to this. He offered to cut his way out and return to Fort Reno (where the wagon train originated) and bring back help. (Earlier, Chaplain White, armed with a six-barrel

Pepperbox handgun, had helped drive some hostiles out of a ravine where they were raining arrows down on the wagon train.) Private William Wallace, who had fought heroically, volunteered to join him. They were given the best horses available and, as night fell, they drove their spurs into their mounts and began a magnificent ride. The Sioux pursued them, however, White and Wallace were able to make their escape.

Before night was fully upon them, sentries spotted a dust cloud approaching the surrounded wagon train. A desperate moan escaped many lips hiding behind the wagons. More Sioux must be arriving, it was thought. Instead, a miracle occurred. Jim Bridger had been sent by Carrington, along with two companies of troops to ascertain the position of the wagon train. At the sight of Bridger and his force, the Sioux slipped away into the darkness. The following day, White and Wallace returned with troops from Fort Reno. The wagon train returned to Fort Reno. After a short rest, it again began its journey towards Fort Phil Kearny, this time with a heavier military escort protecting it. It arrived at Fort Phil Kearny at the end of July.

When they arrived, they quickly saw that their new home was anything but safe. Attacks upon the soldiers and civilians of the fort were almost a daily occurrence. The primary targets of the Sioux and Cheyenne were the wood-cutting parties and any other group that had left the safe confines of Carrington's post. The hostiles used "hit and run" tactics. They would seemingly appear "out of nowhere" and move into attack, firing arrows and bullets at the woodcutters and their escorts, trying to kill as many as possible and possibly stampede their mounts. The soldiers and woodcutters quickly became proficient at "corralling" their wagons and fighting from behind the cover the wagons gave them. Sometimes the attacks would begin at the edge of the pinery. At other times, warriors would "swoop" in just as the woodcutters and their escorts had cleared the main gates of the fort. The warriors also attacked wagon trains traveling along the Bozeman Trail carrying badly needed supplies for Fort Phil

Kearny.

Carrington, despite the repeated attacks on the civilians under his care and his own troops, refused to carry out any offensive action against the hostiles. He felt his priority had to be finishing the construction of Fort Phil Kearny. Winters came early on the Great Plains, and he had women and children he was responsible for, along with his own troops and other civilians. If the fort wasn't finished, many would perish in the elements. He was also concerned about a lack of ammunition and the poor weapons his troops were carrying. He authorized defensive action – that is, soldiers were allowed to defend themselves and the civilians they were protecting. But he would not allow his troops to pursue fleeing hostiles or otherwise take any other offensive action.

At the end of July, Carrington was outraged when he received orders reassigning Captain Hammond and Lieutenant Frederick Phisterer to recruiting duties back in the east. These were two very experienced officers, and Carrington desperately did not want to lose them. Despite written appeals to General Cooke, he was unsuccessful in keeping them.

In August, as the fort was taking shape (despite the best efforts of Red Cloud's warriors) Carrington assigned command of the post to Captain Tenedor Ten Eyck. Carrington had overall command of the entire Second Battalion; however, Ten Eyck had command of the military forces assigned to Fort Phil Kearny. Captain Ten Eyck was a professional engineer, and has been described as very deep, introspective, and exceptionally well read. He was also an alcoholic, and his drinking would eventually destroy his military career.

On September 13[th,] the garrison at Fort Phil Kearny suffered a massive blow. Sioux and Cheyenne warriors "swept in" and destroyed six "mowing machines" (horse drawn machines designed to cut down heavy grass). Even more importantly, they stampeded over 200 head of beef cattle. That cattle was badly needed for food supplies in the upcoming winter. Carrington, desperate to retrieve the cattle, ordered Captain Ten Eyk, along with Lieutenants William Bisbee and Alexander Wands, to lead a small mounted force out of the stockade to attempt to regain the cattle. Despite their best efforts, they were unsuccessful.

Later that day Carrington issued a new order designed to deal with their current, precarious situation. It read as follows:

"Owing to recent depredations of Indians near Fort Philip Kearny, Dak., the post commander (Ten Eyk) will issue such regulation and at once provide such additional escorts for wood trains, guard for stock and hay and steam saw-mills as the chief quartermaster [Brown] may deem essential. He will also give

Instruction, so that upon Indian alarm no troops leave the post without an officer or under the antecedent direction of an officer, and the garrison will be so organized that it may at all times be available and disposable for exterior duty or interior defense.

One relief of the guard will promptly support any picket threatened at night, and the detail on posts should be visited hourly by a non-commissioned officer of the guard between the hours of posting successive reliefs.

Stringent regulations are enjoined to prevent camp rumors and false reports, and any picket or soldier bringing reports of signs of Indian sign or hostilities must be required to report to the post commander or officer of the day or to the nearest commissioned officer in cases of urgent import.

Owing to the non-arrival of corn for the post and the present reduced condition of the public stock, the quartermaster is authorized, upon the approval of the post commander, to purchase sufficient corn for moderate issues, to last until a supply already due, shall arrive, but the issue will be governed by the condition of the stock, and will only be issued to horses unless the same in half ration shall be necessary for such mules as are in daily use and cannot graze or be furnished with hay.

Reports will be made of all Indian depredations, with the results, in order that a proper summary may be sent to department headquarters.

Soldiers while on duty in the timer of elsewhere are forbidden to waste ammunition in hunting, every hour of their time being indispensable in preparing for their own comfort and the well-being of the garrison during the approaching winter. [17]

Were his troops capable of sustained offensive action? The enlisted men were in superb physical shape after months of marching out west and then hard labor building the fort. That being said, Carrington had lost over 100 soldiers due to desertion since the start of the campaign. (One must wonder at the fate of a lone soldier trying to flee to safety in the heart of hostile Sioux territory. Their lifespan was probably measured in a few short days if that.) The ones who remained were excellent workers – but most of them had never fought in battle, and had little experience firing a weapon or riding a horse. Carrington, in fact, had less than 50 rounds of ammunition per soldier, so he could spare little or nothing for proper weapons training. The vast majority of his troops were equipped with Springfield muskets which had been obsolete for years. Only the regimental band had the newer seven-shot Spencer carbines. It thus stands to reason that even if Carrington had been a "bold" combat leader and was eager to strike the hostiles, he wasn't in much of a position to do so successfully.

---

17 Brown, Dee The Fetterman Massacre, pg 122.

On September 23rd, the soldiers at Fort Phil Kearny finally had some combat success against the Sioux. A Sioux war party raided the fort's herd of beef cattle and drove off a large number of cattle. Quartermaster Captain Fred Brown led a counterattack that recovered the cattle and killed six of the Sioux, while suffering no casualties of his own. This was exactly what Carrington's men so badly needed. They had finally struck back at their tormentors and had done so successfully.

The hero was Captain Fred Brown. Brown was considered by all to be warm and friendly, and was an exceptionally capable Quartermaster. He was also an exceptionally hard drinker – like many of the officers of his day. Even though Henry and Margaret Carrington abstained from drinking, they were extremely fond of Captain Brown, as were most other officers and enlisted men at the post.

This first taste of Indian combat seemed to ignite a fire within Brown. He kept his horse saddled at all times and, at the first signal from a sentry that Indians were close, Brown was mounted and leading troops out the gates of the fort. As Quartermaster, the livestock was his responsibility, so he wasn't required to seek Carrington's permission to lead counterattacks out of the fort.

At the end of September, Brown was devastated to receive new orders to report for duty at Fort Laramie. There was little chance of any action at Fort Laramie, and Brown desperately wanted to remain at Fort Phil Kearny. With Carrington's unspoken approval

(since Carrington didn't want to lose this capable officer,) Brown stalled. He claimed he still had inventory to complete and numerous reports to finish. He was determined to stall the transfer as long as possible and perhaps even have it revoked.

Captain Fred Brown

On September 27th, the fort received another blow. Private Patrick Smith and two other soldiers had joined the wood-cutting party, and the three men had worked their way upslope about half a mile from the closest blockhouse. [18] With no warning, dozens of Sioux swarmed between the three men and the main party of woodcutters. The dozen or more men making up the main party of woodcutters immediately flung down their axes, grabbed their rifles, and began firing upon the Sioux. As they fired, they slowly retreated to their blockhouse. Moments after they reached their blockhouse, the two soldiers who had been with Private Smith reached the blockhouse. They reported Private Smith had been killed.

They were incorrect. He had been shot numerous times by arrows. While he was lying in agony, a Sioux leapt off his horse, bent down and scalped him, and left him for dead. Smith, however, was made of very tough material. Bleeding profusely, he broke the arrows off so he could crawl, and pulled himself across the ground until he reached the blockhouse and was able to bang on the door. His horrified comrades pulled him inside, put him in a bunk, and sent a heavily armed party to the fort requesting medical aid be sent quickly.

After scalping Smith, the same group of Sioux attacked the four soldiers or pickets assigned to Pilot Hill. Captain Brown and Lieutenant John Adair led a heavily armed party of 20 troopers out of the fort in aid of the pickets. Brown's force successfully cut off the Sioux attack, rescuing the pickets, and driving the attackers off.

Shortly after the Sioux were driven off, Private Smith was brought by wagon into the fort. Surgeon Edwin Reid was able to save the young man's life although he wrote later that he had tremendous difficulty

---

18 Blockhouses were solid structures built from logs to which the woodcutter could retreat to in time of danger. They had small slit windows that could be used to fire upon the enemy.

removing one particular arrow from the private's chest.

News about the plight of Private Smith spread around Fort Phil Kearny like wildfire. Everyone could imagine the young private, with broken arrows embedded in his body, skin hanging in strips from his head down across his face dragging himself across the ground towards the blockhouse. The mood of the soldiers posted there was that of "red rage." Smith was popular and although he would live, his comrades vowed that there would be revenge.

Chaplain White (who had so distinguished himself during the fighting at Crazy Woman Creek two months before) overheard numerous soldiers plan an attack that night on a party of friendly Cheyenne who were camped near the fort. (Many of the soldiers posted at Fort Phil Kearny by now believed that there was no such thing as a "friendly Indian.") White immediately reported this news to Carrington. Carrington and Captain Ten Eyck led a force out of the compound with a plan to surround the Cheyenne village and prevent an attack upon it. They actually surprised over 90 troopers who had slipped out of the fort and were preparing their own attack upon the friendly Cheyenne. That force scattered when they heard Carrington's orders to disperse.

By early October, mornings were met with heavy frost on the ground. There was thin ice forming in the nearby river. The ice would melt by late morning, but the warnings were clear. The dreaded Great Plains winter was rapidly approaching. Carrington knew this, and was furiously driving his men to get the fort built.

The day after the Carrington prevented his men from attacking the Cheyenne village, he met in his office with Lieutenants Bisbee, Wands, and Captain Ten Eyck. Bisbee was furious and he went after his commanding officer in a rage:

"Sir with all due respect you should have let the men take care of those Cheyenne last night. An Injun is an Injun. There is no such thing as a friendly one. If you had let us hit them the word would have gotten back to Red Cloud to leave us alone. We are just sitting here getting hit day after day. It is driving the men insane. We are just waiting to be killed. You have to turn us loose!"

Wands, while also angry, was more tempered, "I agree that the men are frustrated and angry. But I for one am not sure that we are capable of much offensive action. The troops here are young, raw, and have had little drill. They are more construction laborers then they are soldiers." He turned to Carrington and said, "Sir, you have to give us time to drill the men. We can't sit back and simply be targets. But you have to give us the chance to turn these men into soldiers. Otherwise sir, we will all die here."

Carrington coldly stared at his officers. Bisbee and Wands returned his glare. Captain Ten Eyck looked down at the floor. Carrington began, "Gentlemen I appreciate the passion you feel. But let me be clear. What happened last night will never happen again. Offensive action against the Indians will be conducted only upon direct orders by myself. And those orders will not be given until this fort is 100% complete. Winter is coming and we have a very short period of time to get this work done. That is my priority and will remain my priority. The regular drilling of troops will commence only after this post is complete. Am I clear?"

Bisbee and Wands looked sullenly at their commanding officer but nodded. Ten Eyck quietly responded, "Very clear sir."

Carrington then said, "Very well then. We have a busy day ahead of ourselves. You are dismissed."

Bisbee and Wands left Carrington's office in a rage. Bisbee turned to his colleague and said, "Alex, do you know who we need here?"

Wands looked at Bisbee and answered, "No Will, who do we need, other than a new commanding officer with some courage?"

Bisbee smiled and said, "Will, we need Fetterman. God, that man can fight. He is a true soldier, he is. He could show Carrington what it means to be a soldier and I guarantee you he could whip any bunch of heathen Sioux."

Wands looked at Bisbee and smiled. He then said; "I haven't met Fetterman but I have heard all about him. Who knows – he is part of our regiment and Washington may just send him here when they realize Carrington can't or won't fight."

On October 6, another event occurred which would, within two months, add to the legend of Fort Phil Kearny. On that day a large wagon train operated by a contractor arrived with badly needed supplies. Among its contents were over 60,000 rounds of Springfield ammunition, and bushels of corn that the contractor was willing to sell for the army mounts. Joining the wagon train was an ambulance. In the ambulance were two surgeons, a young cavalry lieutenant and his wife.

LIEUTENANT GEORGE GRUMMOND

The lieutenant was a young "dashing" Civil War hero by the name of George Washington Grummond. He was joined by his beautiful, young and very pregnant wife Frances. Grummond had served with distinction during the Civil War, rising through the ranks from Sergeant to a brevet rank of Lieutenant Colonel. And yet there was a dark side to this young man as author Shannon Smith described:

"Closer scrutiny reveals an unseemly background of aggression, cruelty, and ungentlemanly conduct. His rapid promotions were based on near-reckless bravery in battle. In August 1864, after several incidents in which his irrational zeal for conflict and acts of brutality – all while intoxicated – imperiled his troops, a group of his junior officers petitioned the adjutant general to investigate whether Grummond was fit to command." [19]

The result of this petition was a general court martial where Grummond was found guilty of threatening to shoot a fellow officer and of actually shooting an unarmed civilian. For that Grummond received a public reprimand but retained his rank.

Less than a month after that embarrassment, Grummond was again in "hot water." While serving in Tennessee under Brigadier General Robert Granger, Grummond was given orders to bring his cavalry unit to a particular position at a designated time. Grummond instead rushed his unit forward, three hours earlier than expected. By doing so he alerted his Confederate foes of the Union army's plans, and then had to send a courier to Granger for assistance as he found himself embroiled in a savage battle with Confederate units that

---

[19] Smith, Shannon, Give Me Eighty Good Men, pg 66.

outnumbered his own. Granger, after the battle, wrote a scathing report condemning Grummond's actions.

On several other occasions in 1865 Grummond was sanctioned for "jumping the gun" and rushing his troops recklessly into battle before other Union forces were prepared to support him. Nobody questioned George Grummond's bravery. Many questioned his judgment.

Grummond's poor judgment was also reflected in his personal life. At the outbreak of the Civil War, the 26 year old Grummond was married to a 20 year old woman named Delia and they resided in Detroit. They had one child. In 1863 Delia gave birth to a second child. But by that time Grummond, while on duty in the South had met a breathtakingly beautiful "southern belle" named Frances Courtney. Upon meeting Ms. Courtney, Grummond ceased his efforts to support his family back in Detroit. His conduct was deemed so outrageous for an "officer and a gentleman" that the courts granted Delia a divorce (divorce being very unusual in Victorian times) plus full custody of their children. They also ordered Grummond to pay her a sum of $2,000 in quarterly installments over the next year. How he was supposed to do this wasn't apparent as that sum of alimony was greater than his annual salary. Seemingly unfazed by the public outrage his conduct created, Grummond married Frances Courtney on September 3, 1865 – 20 days before his divorce was finalized.

Tales of his most scandalous behavior hadn't reached Fort Phil Kearny and so it wasn't long before the handsome Grummond and his beautiful young wife were the most popular young couple in the officers' social gatherings.

Before the Grummonds could become the "light" of the Fort Phil Kearny social scene, Frances Grummond received a terrible shock upon arrival at the fort. The ambulance she and her husband were travelling in closed in on the main gates when they suddenly halted. As she wrote in her diary:

"We moved towards the stockade", she wrote, 'but just before entering a halt was made, and I looked eagerly for the occasion of the delay. It almost took my breath away for a strange feeling of apprehension came over me. We had halted to give passage to a wagon, escorted by a guard from the wood train...In the wagon was the scalped and naked body of one of their comrades...My whole being seemed to be absorbed in the one desire – an agonized but unuttered cry, "Let me get within the gate"...That strange feeling of apprehension never left me, enhanced as it was by my delicate condition." [20]

---

20 Brown, Dee, *The Fetterman Massacre,* pg 126.

Frances Grummond—A gentle Easterner, she became a living epic of all the West could deal out to a woman.

Frances Grummond

Lieutenant George W. Grummond

The victim whose bloody body so traumatized Frances Grummond, was photographer Ridgeway Glover. Glover had traveled to Fort Phil Kearny on the same wagon train that was embroiled in the battle at Crazy Woman Creek. He narrowly escaped death there. Once reaching his destination, Glover would disappear for days at a time into the mountains and bush surrounding the fort. He was warned repeatedly not to wander off alone, for it meant almost certain death. Glover, who had long yellow/blonde hair, joked that the hostiles would leave him alone as they would think he was a Mormon. (Why he thought the Sioux would leave a Mormon alone is unknown.)

On the day in question Glover was taking photos with the wood-cutting party. He decided to pack up his equipment and travel back alone to the fort. The woodcutters pleaded with him to remain with them. Glover simply laughed them off. He never made the fort. The following day a mounted detail commanded by Lieutenant Bisbee found his naked, scalped body. Bisbee reported that Glover was found lying face down. That was a symbol the Sioux left of a man who didn't die bravely. Glover's photographic equipment was smashed. There has never been any record of the photographs that he took ever being found.

On the same day that the Grummonds arrived, Colonel Carrington received disturbing news from Jim Bridger. Bridger reported that local Crow Indians had told him that there were now over 500 lodges of hostile Sioux, all armed with rifles, camped along the Tongue River, well within striking distance of Carrington's post. Carrington was frustrated beyond belief by this point. He had received numerous dispatches from General Cooke criticizing him for inaction against the hostiles. And yet he had still not received the promised reinforcements he so desperately needed, as well as forage for his horses. The contractor with whom the Grummonds had traveled had sold Captain Brown bushels of badly needed corn, but that simply wasn't enough if Carrington was expected to launch offensive action. And now with the news that Bridger had brought, Carrington knew there were even more hostiles in the area. How was he to launch offensive action against the hostiles with ill fed horses and a lack of ammunition? And on top of that – get the fort 100% completed before the first of the winter snows arrived! These were tasks that were seemingly utterly impossible to accomplish in Carrington's mind.

The life that Frances Grummond encountered at Fort Phil Kearny was radically different from that of what she had experienced in Tennessee, and truth be told, different from what any of the officers' wives had experienced. Instead of servants cooking and cleaning for them in beautiful, well-made quarters, they now had to cook and clean and live in hastily built wooden structures. They sewed clothing for themselves, their husbands and children. On warm days, there could be a game of croquet to entertain them. In the evenings, they would put on their nicest clothing, their husbands would don their dress uniforms, and couples would socialize. There would be games such as charades, readings of any new books that had arrived at the fort, and the regimental band would entertain with music. Sunday would be devoted to Chapel and the worship of God. But there was never a sense of peace. Always lurking outside of the stockade walls was the reality of the Sioux and Cheyenne, poised to attack.

For the troops, food was fairly uninspiring and monotonous. Army regulations of the day dictated that the daily ration be:

"…three-fourths of a pound of pork or bacon, or one and a fourth pound of fresh or salt beef; eighteen ounces of bread or flour, or 12 ounces of hard bread, or one and a fourth pound corn meal; and at the rate to one hundred rations of eight quarts of beans, or in lieu thereof ten pounds of rice, or lieu thereof twice per week one hundred and fifty ounces of desiccated potatoes, and one hundred ounces of mixed vegetables; ten pounds of coffee, or in lieu thereof one and one half pound of tea; fifteen pounds of sugar; four quarts of vinegar...." [21]

At the end of October 1866, the first and the last bright moments at Fort Phil Kearny occurred. The weather, while being cold in the mornings, was overall very pleasant in the day. The air was described as crisp and cold, with the sky being an "incredible blue." Carrington declared that October 30 and 31 would be "holidays" to celebrate the completion of the construction of Fort Phil Kearny. Soldiers as well as officers were issued new uniforms that had been carefully hoarded. Halyards were installed on the new 124 foot flagpole. Many officers moved from tents into their newly constructed quarters on "Officers Row." Frances Grummond was very pleased with her large double bed that had been constructed by the fort's carpenters.

The fort's sutler, a man named Judge Kinney, handed out gingersnap cookies and sugar balls to the various children in the fort. Troops formed up into companies for inspection, and finally Colonel Carrington and the other senior officers, along with Chaplain White and Judge Kinney, mounted a hastily constructed platform and faced the troops. Judge Kinney read a poem, and then Chaplain White offered a prayer. Finally, Colonel Carrington began speaking to the crowd assembled in front of him:

"Fifteen weeks have passed, varied by many skirmishes and both day and night alarms...In every work done your arms have been at hand. In the pine tracts or hay fields, on picket or general guard duty, no one has failed to find a constant exposure to some hostile shaft, and to feel that a cunning adversary was watching every chance to harass and kill...

The steam whistle and the rattle of the mower have followed your

---

[21] Murray, Robert "Military Posts in the Powder River Country of Wyoming, 1865-1894," University of Nebraska Press, Lincoln, 1968, pg 19.

steps in this westward march of empire. You have built a central post that will bear comparison with any for security, completeness, and adaption to the ends in view, wherever the other may be located, or however long in erection.

Surrounded by temptation to hunt the choicest game, and allured by tales of golden treasure just beyond you, you have spared your powder for your foes, and have given the labor of your hands to your proper work. Passing from guard- watching to fatigue-work, and after one night in bed, often disturbed, returning to your post as entry, attempting with success all trades and callings, and handling the broad-axe and hammer, the saw and the chisel, with the same success as that which you have sped the bullet, your work has proven how well deserved was the confidence I reposed in all of you…

And now this day, laying aside the worn and tattered garments, which have done their part during weeks of toil and struggle, the veteran battalion of the 18th Infantry…puts on its fresh full-dress attire for muster and review.

The crowning office, without which you would regard your work as scarcely begun, is now to be performed, and to its fulfillment I assign soldiers; neither discharging the duty myself, nor delegating it to some brother officer; but some veteran soldier of good desert shall share with a sergeant from each of their companies, and the worthy man whose work rises high above us, the honor of raising our new and beautiful garrison flag to the top of the handsomest flagstaff in America.

It is the first full garrison flag that has floated between the Platte and Montana.

With music and the roar of cannon we shall greet its unfoldings.

This day shall be a holiday, and a fresh starting point for future endeavor.

And yet all is not said that I wish to say! While we exalt the national standard, and rejoice in its glory and its power, let us not forget the true source of that glory and power...

Let me, then, ask all, with uncovered heads and grateful hearts, to pause in our act of consecration, while the chaplain shall invoke God's own blessing upon that act; so that while this banner rises heavenward, and so shall rise with each recurring sun, all hearts shall rise to the throne of the Infinite, and for this day, its duties and its pleasures, we shall become better men and better soldiers of the great Republic." [22]

With that, Lieutenant Adair gave a signal and a group of sergeants and enlisted men assembled around the flagstaff.. Chaplain White offered a brief prayer, then a succession of commands rang out: "Attention! Present arms! Play! Hoist! Fire!"

Frances Grummond described the scene: "With the simultaneous snap of presented arms in salute, the long roll of the combined drum-corps was followed by the full band playing the 'Star Spangled Banner', the guns opened fire, and the magnificent flag with its thirty-six-foot fly and its twenty-foot hoist slowly rose to masthead and was broken out in glorious flame of red, white, and blue!" [23]

Once the flag was raised, the assembly was dismissed, and the officers and enlisted men who were not on duty were free to enjoy the day either amongst each other or, for those who had brought their families, with them.

Colonel Carrington and his wife Margaret walked through the post greetings others.   She turned to her husband and said, "Henry

---

[22] Brown, Dee, "The Fetterman Massacre" pg 153-155

[23] Ibid, pg. 155

you did what many thought could not be done. You have built this simply magnificent fort in the heart of what must be the most hostile territory in our nation. I am so proud of you."

"Thank you my dear," Carrington responded. "This was my biggest challenge and I met it. Now if only we could receive the reinforcements and ammunition that keep being promised to me. Then maybe I could show the men here that not only can I build a fort – but that I can also fight. After all I am a soldier."

On that last day of October 1866, Carrington had under his command at Fort Phil Kearny a force of approximately 360 officers and enlisted men. More reinforcements were on the way however and they would help ensure Fort Phil Kearny's place in history forever.

FETTERMAN ARRIVES

The high spirits of the previous day ended on the evening of November 1st. That evening, a Montana-bound civilian wagon train camped outside the gates of Fort Phil Kearny. As many of the men in the train sat around open fires playing cards (they believed that the extreme proximity of the fort protected them), Sioux and Cheyenne warriors slipped in close and opened fire upon them. Immediately three white men dropped down to the ground wounded – one fatally.

As the troops in the fort grabbed their weapons at the sounds of gunfire, the civilians in the wagon train began returning fire. As they did so, signal fires began appearing in the hills around the fort. Very quickly, Fort Phil Kearny appeared to be surrounded by countless fires blazing in the hills circling the outpost. Through the dim light of the flames could be seen the specter of seemingly thousands of hostile Sioux and Cheyenne dancing around the flames. Carrington ran out of his quarters at the sounds of the commotions and peered through his binoculars at the fires surrounding the post. He looked at his wife Margaret and commented, " My god we really are posted in Hell."

He then turned to his gunnery crew manning one of the posts howitzers. "Men fire at will at those savages you can see through the flames in the hills," he barked.

The howitzers sent high explosive shells whistling amongst the Sioux and Cheyenne. The warriors dove for cover as red hot, razor sharp shrapnel exploded amongst them, some of which tore into their bodies, ripping them apart. The shells also exploded amongst the flames, extinguishing many of the roaring fires. (As well as more than one human life.)

Carrington then ordered a "skirmish party" (a small armed military patrol) out of the gates, however the soldiers were unable to find any trace of the warriors who had attacked the wagon train.

Two days later, 63 men of Company C, 2nd US Cavalry, commanded by Lieutenant Horatio Bingham, rode through the gates of Fort Phil Kearny. The troops of Company C were armed with obsolete breech loading Starr carbines. Accompanying Company C was Captain William Judd Fetterman. The most legendary combat leader in the history of the 18th Infantry Regiment had arrived.

Captain Fetterman had been assigned to administrative duties in the East when he was advised of a large reorganization within the army. The 1866 Army Reorganization Act assigned Fetterman to Fort Phil Kearny, where he was to supersede Colonel Henry Carrington as commander of the post in the New Year. The Second Battalion of the 18th Infantry Regiment was going to form the nucleus of the new 27th Infantry Regiment and be commanded by Fetterman. Carrington was to be moved to a new post (Fort Casper) and be placed in command of the First Battalion of the 18th Infantry. Until Carrington moved to his post in 1867, the two men would have to co-exist with Carrington as the commander.

Carrington had mixed feelings about this. "Margaret," he said to his wife. "I feel as I am being moved due to some failure on my part here. But I have built this magnificent outpost in such harsh and trying circumstances. I am criticized time and time again – even by my own officers for not striking at the hostiles. Yet I don't have the men and ammunition to do so successfully."

Margaret Carrington looked at her husband. "Henry you know you have done what you can. Let Fetterman see what it is really like out here. He'll find out soon enough and when he does you will be vindicated."

Also joining Fetterman and the company of cavalry were Captain James W. Powell and Major Henry Almstedt. There was also a mailbag with dispatches for Carrington from General Cooke. Cooke chastised Carrington for the few dispatches he received from Fort Phil Kearny (Cooke seemed to have no idea of the difficulty in sending and receiving mail in this region) and he urged Carrington to take offensive action against the hostiles.

When Fetterman dismounted after entering the post, he was quickly and warmly met by his old Civil War compatriots Captain Fred Brown and Lieutenant William Bisbee. Lieutenant George Grummond quickly introduced himself to Fetterman and remarked, "Sir, I am glad that we now have a true soldier in command here. It will be an honor to fight under your command."

Fetterman smiled and responded, "Lieutenant it will be an honor to command you and your men. And I assure you that together we will make Red Cloud very sorry."

That evening the sutler Judge Kinney sold vast amounts of whiskey as Fetterman, Bisbee, Brown, Grummond and Ten Eyck gathered to reacquaint themselves with one another and catch up on the news from back East.

Fetterman turned to his old friend Fred Brown and asked, "Fred tell me the truth. What is the situation here? The talk back East is that Carrington is a timid, old fool. That he is scared to fight. Is that true? I served with him back East at Camp Thomas. He was a very able administrator there but he never fought. "

Brown spat some tobacco juice into a spittoon and gulped some whiskey. He then responded, "Will, Carrington is an old woman. He is gutless. He won't fight. Even worse he won't let us drill the troops. The men spend all their time on construction duties and most of them couldn't hit the side of a barn with their rifle. He can run an office but he sure as hell can't command fighting troops."

Lieutenant Bisbee added, "Captain he is right. My men haven't drilled in weeks. We need a couple of hard weeks of drilling and then by god turn us loose! We'll send Red Cloud and all of his warriors to hell!"

Fetterman nodded. "Okay men," he began. "I will deal with Carrington tomorrow. I will personally lead the drilling of the troops. We have to get them squared away and fast. I am not going to spend the winter here as a sitting target. Once the men are ready we are going to take the fight to those red bastards. They will wish they were never born when I am through with them. But until then I do have a plan. Some of us are ready and able to fight right now. And I know just how to do it."

With that Fetterman quietly discussed his idea with Brown and Grummond, who both quickly nodded their heads in approval.

The next morning Fetterman was in Carrington's office presenting his plan on drilling the troops and his idea for an immediate, quick strike at the hostiles. His plan was to take a small, heavily armed detachment out at night and conceal them in a thicket of woods opposite the fort. Then they'd leave some mules tied to stakes between the thicket and the fort as bait. No Sioux or Cheyenne worth their salt would turn down the opportunity to steal some of the white man's livestock!

Carrington felt it was very risky, but he reluctantly gave Fetterman permission to try. That night, Fetterman led a detachment into the thicket. They waited for hours. However, the hostiles left the mules alone. Just as Fetterman led his sleepy troops back into the fort, Sioux and Cheyenne warriors struck the opposite side of the fort, and stampeded a small herd of cattle owned by civilian James Wheatley. Fetterman was furious. He'd been at Fort Phil Kearny less than three days and already he had egg on his face.

Fetterman was able to convince Carrington to allow him to begin drilling the troops. The fort was to all extents and purposes built, and now it was time to turn the troops from laborers into true soldiers. On a daily basis the parade ground was full of drilling troops and officers and sergeants putting them through their paces. Fetterman was a hard task master. He knew he needed trained troops to be successful, so he drove his men unmercifully. It wasn't long until they were responding to his directives and the confidence level of Captain William Fetterman rose. He had come to Fort Phil Kearny contemptuous of the Plains Indians. He knew in his heart that they could not fight and defeat trained, disciplined troops. His troops were quickly becoming the force he needed to unleash on Red Cloud and his followers.

That same week in which Fetterman arrived, Jim Bridger returned to the post after conferring with various Crows at Fort C.F. Smith. The Crows advised Bridger that the Arapaho had joined with the Sioux and Cheyenne and were determined to wipe Fort Phil Kearny off the map. More and more hostiles were pouring into the area. Carrington's heart grew cold at Bridger's news. He began to wonder if he and his wife would leave Fort Phil Kearny alive come the New Year.

On Sunday, November 11th, an incident occurred on the parade ground that sent tremors through the post. Company E, commanded by Lieutenant Bisbee, was forming up for guard duty when Private John Burke joined the ranks late. Bisbee, who had a reputation as a harsh disciplinarian, exploded in a profanity-laced tirade at the young private and ordered Sergeant Garrett to discipline him. When Burke heard Bisbee's orders, he cursed. Garrett responded by clubbing him in the head with the butt of his musket, fracturing his skull. Colonel Carrington, along with his wife and several other couples, witnessed this event while on their way to church. He was appalled at what he saw and heard, and after church services he drafted General Order Number 38 which ordered his officers to practice humane discipline and refrain from vulgar and profane language. Lieutenant Bisbee was ordered to post the orders throughout the fort, which led to an even deeper divide between Carrington and most of his officers.

That evening, Fetterman, Captains Brown and Powell, along with Lieutenants Bisbee and Grummond, sat around the sutler's bar drinking Judge Kinney's whiskey and cursing Carrington.

"Bloody old woman he is," grumbled Fetterman. "Here you are just enforcing discipline in the ranks and he goes and cuts you right off at the knees. Don't worry – I'll be running this post in less than two months. It will be very different then."

The other officers nodded. ""That can't happen soon enough Will," answered Fred Brown. "We've been sitting out here getting our hides tanned while that old fool does nothing. I don't think he'd fight if the goddamn savages were pouring over the walls. Hell with what he showed us today he may even greet the savages as they poured over the walls!"

Fetterman smiled and said, "Don't worry Fred. Soon we'll all get our chance to take Red Cloud's scalp."

By now the winter was really setting in upon the inhabitants of Fort Phil Kearny. For people like Frances Grummond, it was something she was not prepared for. Growing up in the South, winter was at worst, a period of time with cooler temperatures and the very odd snow fall. Here on the western frontier it was something else altogether. Temperatures dropped below freezing, snow fell in abundant amounts, and the wind howled leading to wind chill factors well below zero degrees. The bitter winds found their way through the chinks in the hastily constructed buildings. These were the days before insulation and central heating so the only heat came from wood burning stoves and fire places that had to kept burning 24 hours per day. People slept with multiple layers of blankets on them to keep from freezing. There were no modern clothing materials such as Gor-Tex for people to wear to stay warm and dry. The clothing of the time was limited to multiple layers of cotton; wool and animal furs which were useless if they became damp or wet. Bathing required men going to Big Piney Creek (at the same time risking attack), using axes to cut through the ice and filling buckets with freezing water and chunks of ice, and bringing those same buckets back to the fort that then had to be heated over fires before being used for bathing. Needless to say a weekly bath was a true luxury!

The women and children were also suffering from "cabin fever." Due to the omnipresent threat of attack no woman or child had been allowed outside the gates of the stockade since October 31st. The children were kept busy by school lessons however their ability to play and keep entertained was very limited as the fort was not overly large. With sections of the fort closed off due to military necessity, areas where children could play outside were very restricted. Women cleaned, cooked and entertained each other but even with those activities immense boredom followed by terror for the lives of their spouses, as the wood cutting parties were regularly attacked, took a tremendous mental toll on them all. It was for all a very hard and at times cruel life.

Ten days later, Fetterman had his first contact with the hostiles. He, along with his close friend Lieutenant Bisbee, joined the escort party to the pinery. While riding ahead of the escort party, they stopped to water their horses. Suddenly shots rang out. At Bisbee's urging, he and Fetterman took cover. A lone warrior then came out of the bush and taunted the officers. Fetterman started to rise up and draw his revolver. Bisbee grabbed his arm, pointed at the thicket of trees ahead of them and said, "Will stay down. He isn't the only one in there. There are probably a hundred or more in the bush there. If you go after him you'll never come out alive."

Before Fetterman could decide whether or not to take Bisbee's advice, the rest of the escort party galloped up, and then the thicket in front of them erupted with dozens of warriors. They shook their weapons at the small group of soldiers and galloped off. Fetterman cursed under his breath. He had now had two opportunities to show he could fight and defeat the hostiles. In neither case did he lose – but nor did he win.

Four days later, Carrington shook his head at yet another dispatch from General Cooke. It read:

"Colonel: You are hereby instructed that so soon as the troops and stores are covered from the weather, to turn your earnest attention the possibility of striking the hostile band of Indians by surprise in their winter camps, as intimated in telegram of 27 September ultimo from these headquarters.

An extraordinary effort in winter, when the Indian horses are unserviceable, it is believed, should be followed by more success than can be accomplished by large expeditions in the summer, when the Indians can so easily scatter into deserts and mountain hiding places almost beyond pursuit.

Four companies of infantry will be available, besides some cavalry. You have a large arrear of murderous and insulting attacks by the savages upon emigrant trains and troops to settle, and you are ordered, if there prove to be any promise of success, to conduct or to send under another officer, such an expedition." [24]

Carrington felt despair when he read the orders from General Cooke. His one company of cavalry, which had just recently arrived,

---

24 Ibid pg 170-171

was in constant use as an escort for the woodcutters. They were armed with obsolete Starr carbines. His infantry, which was being rapidly turned into effective troops through the constant drilling by Fetterman, was still poorly armed with Springfield muskets. Carrington had requested an additional 100 Springfields to replace broken, worn out weapons. They had yet to arrive. Carrington could only shake his head and think that if General Cooke had any idea of what shape Carrington's troops and equipment were in he'd refrain from these ridiculous orders.

On December 2^{nd,} Carrington's situation became even worse. Lieutenant Bisbee had received new orders to report to General Cooke to serve as his personal aide-de-camp. Bisbee was no supporter of Carrington; however, he was a capable and experienced combat officer, and his departure would leave another hole in Carrington's forces.

Four days later on December 6th, Carrington finally went on the offensive. Pickets on Pilot Hill began waving flags, indicating that the woodcutting party was under attack. Fetterman led a force of 30 cavalry, along with Lieutenant Horatio Bingham, out of the fort and to the west towards the woodcutting party. He was then to drive the hostiles north of the Sullivant Hills to where a force commanded by Carrington himself, and 21 mounted infantry soldiers, would be waiting to smash them. Joining Carrington would be Lieutenants Grummond and Wands, although Wands would be delayed by a broken saddle and would end up joining Fetterman's command. Captain Fred Brown, as was his habit was eager to fight and he, on his own initiative, also joined Fetterman's command.

Before setting out, Margaret Carrington turned to her husband and said, "Henry must you go? You work in an office and are a lawyer and an engineer. Leave the fighting to Fetterman and Grummond. They want to fight and they are experienced at it. You could die out there."

Henry Carrington looked sadly at his wife. "Margaret my dear", he said. "I have to go today. All the men think I am a coward and I don't know how to fight. At least once an officer must prove himself in combat. If I don't go out there, I will lose my men and thus my command. They will not follow me and getting them to carry out any orders will be almost impossible. You must see that I have to go."

Margaret Carrington began crying but she nodded her head. "I understand Henry" she replied. "But please return home to me."

Henry Carrington looked tenderly at her. "I will my dear. I will see you soon."

With that the two separate commands left Fort Phil Kearny. Fetterman led his command to the woodcutting party where they encountered over 100 hostile Sioux and Cheyenne warriors. Despite outnumbering Fetterman's command by over 3-1, the hostiles retreated in the direction of where Carrington was rushing to position his troops.

Fetterman, seeing his enemy fleeing, turned to Captain Fred Brown, and said, "I knew it Fred. They are cowards! They won't stand and fight. Let's get them!"

With that Fetterman gave the orders to pursue the fleeing hostiles. As they galloped in hot pursuit many of the troopers fired their revolvers at the fleeing Indians. Lieutenant Wands screamed, "Cease fire! They are too far away. You are just wasting ammunition."

They galloped down a steep hill and when they reached the bottom, seemingly hundreds of Sioux and Cheyenne sprang out from behind rocks and from deep grass where they had hidden. Instantly the air was filled with flying arrows. Fetterman was too experienced to panic, but he knew his command was in mortal danger. He ordered his troops to dismount and fight on foot. Before that command could be carried out, Lieutenant Bingham pointed to a gap in the mass of hostiles and screamed, "Come on boys. Let's get the hell out of here!"

With that Bingham led twenty of his cavalry troopers in a full-fledged retreat towards the fort. Fetterman was stunned. However, he aimed his rifle at the remaining ten cavalry troopers and roared, "Goddamn it! Next one of you who runs I'll shoot him myself. We stand and fight!"

With that Fetterman and his troops kneeled down and began firing into the masses of warriors. The hostiles were firing arrows at Fetterman's command but scoring very few hits. The battle raged for close to 20 minutes when Carrington's force appeared in the distance. Momentarily, the firing stopped as both parties assumed Carrington was coming to Fetterman's aid. They were incorrect, however. Carrington had not seen nor heard Fetterman's engagement and was simply moving towards the pre-arranged rendezvous point. When Carrington moved on, Fetterman and the hostiles resumed their combat.

Carrington, meanwhile, was having his own difficulties. After departing the fort, he had attempted to cross the frozen Big Piney Creek when his horse threw him and Carrington crashed through the ice into three feet of freezing water. Carrington emerged from the freezing water "soaked to the bone." Lieutenant Grummond, concerned about the well-being of his commanding officer (and probably as well eager to get the inexperienced Carrington "out of his way") said, "Sir, you could catch pneumonia. Please go back to the fort and dry off and get dry clothes on. We'll carry on without you."

Carrington, embarrassed at his fall on his first combat mission, shook his head. "We will carry on Lieutenant. I will not go back as the men will think I am a coward and I most certainly am not. I am in command here and will remain with you. Thank you for your concern however we have a mission that we need to complete. "

With that, Carrington's command again moved forward. Just as they moved across the creek, several warriors became visible in the distance. Without any directives from Carrington, Grummond and three other soldiers galloped after them. Carrington yelled several times to Grummond to cease his pursuit and return, before finally sending an orderly after them with orders to break off the pursuit and return. The orderly, however, was not able to catch up with Grummond. The brash young lieutenant disappeared from view.

As Carrington continued to advance, he came upon a detachment of Lieutenant Bingham's cavalry, who had abandoned Fetterman. Carrington demanded to know where Bingham was. He was advised that the lieutenant had advanced ahead in the direction where Grummond had galloped off to. Before Carrington could fully comprehend that bit of news, his command was suddenly blocked by the appearance of over 100 hostiles in front of him. Carrington ordered bugler Adolf Metzger to sound "Recall" and began deploying his troops in skirmish formation. The crisp, clear notes of the bugle sounded through the bitter cold air, followed by the crash of heavy gunfire from Carrington's troops. As his men pumped volleys of fire into the massed warriors, Carrington thought to himself, "Well Henry you wanted to taste combat. Now you have it. Please god don't allow me make a mistake that will get my men killed."

Private James McGuire was thrown from his horse when the animal collapsed from mortal wounds. As McGuire struggled to get clear of the beast, a Sioux warrior charged him waving a war club. Carrington instantly moved between the two and killed the warrior with his revolver. Colonel Henry Carrington was demonstrating that he wasn't a coward and that he could command troops in combat.

Carrington by now had all his men dismounted and pouring heavy fire into the onrushing hostiles. Starr carbines and Springfield muskets belched fire and smoke. Carrington ran from man to man bellowing orders and encouragement.

At the other end of the battlefield, Fetterman and his command were on the move. The hostiles had broken off their attacks on his force to engage Carrington's command. As soon as Fetterman heard firing from Carrington's position he immediately did what all officers are trained to do - that is immediately advance to the sound of the firing. "Fred, Alex, let's get the men moving" he yelled at Captain Brown and Lieutenant Wands. "That fool Carrington is engaged and he'll get all his men killed if we don't save him!"

With that the officers got the men into formation and they moved quickly towards the sound of Carrington's battle.

With the appearance of Fetterman's command, the hostiles engaged with Carrington retreated, allowing Fetterman to unite his command with that of his commanding officer.

The question of where Lieutenants Grummond and Bingham were still had to be answered. And to that came the sound of firing and screams of soldiers and Sioux and Cheyenne to the front of the now united command. That question was now answered.

Grummond, along with a small group of cavalry, caught up to Bingham, who was pursuing a single fleeing warrior. As the soldiers galloped into Peno Valley, dozens of concealed Sioux and Cheyenne sprang out at them. Lieutenant Bingham dropped from his saddle shot through the head. The warriors charged the mounted troopers, trying to lasso (and thus capture) the big army horses and knock the mounted troopers from them. Lieutenant Gummond drew his saber, and with a blood crazed, almost psychotic look on his face, began slashing his way out of the morass of hostiles.

"Cmon you bastards," he screamed. 'Here is some cold steel for you heathen savages as I send you to hell! Taste this," he shrieked as he deftly cleaved off the arm of one Sioux who had charged him waving a tomahawk. The warrior looked stunned at his amputated arm lying in the snow and then collapsed. The other mounted soldiers, unable to fire their weapons in such close quarters, used their rifles as clubs as they smashed in enemy skulls in an effort to fight their way out. Grummond, cackling almost insanely now, and filled with an unquenchable "blood rage," brutally decapitated a charging Cheyenne and slashed the throat of another Sioux. The Indians then backed away from the whirling dervish of razor sharp steel. Grummond used that slight hesitation to spur his mount forward. He roared, "Let's go boys," and he, along with three other troopers, charged out of the ambush. They took off at full gallop back towards Carrington's position with about 10 enemies in hot pursuit.

As Grummond's force reached the Carrington/Fetterman position, the pursuing hostile warriors broke off contact and retreated. Grummond rode directly up to his commanding officer and, shaking from the adrenalin pumping through his system, screamed at Carrington, "You stupid old fool! Why didn't you follow me? You left us there to fend for ourselves!"

Colonel Carrington reeled as if he had been shot, as he was subjected to Grummond's tirade. Barely keeping himself under control, the gentlemanly Carrington calmly responded, "Lieutenant you are way out of line. Say another word and I'll have you slapped in irons and confined to the guardhouse."

Grummond was shaking – his body visibly vibrating from the adrenalin and rage running through him. Fetterman used this moment to grab the lieutenant and pull him away from Carrington. Fetterman leaned into the out of control young officer and said, "Lieutenant, shut up now or your career is over. Shut up and move away with me and I'll patch things up. Say another word and it's out of my hands."

Grummond slowly swung his horse around and moved away from the shocked colonel. Carrington regained his composure and ordered a search for Lieutenant Bingham and Sergeant Gideon Bowers, who was now, reported missing as well.

The two were found very close to each other. Bingham was found shot through the head and his body bristling with over 50 arrows in it. Bowers was found barely alive. His head had been cleaved opened by a Sioux war club. Before dying, he gasped out that he had killed three enemy warriors with his revolver. The blood trails leading away from his body (Sioux and Cheyenne if they could, always took their dead with them) seemed to support Bowers' version of events.

Carrington's troops gathered up the bodies of Bingham and Gideon, and the command slowly made their way back to Fort Phil Kearny. It was a somber homecoming for the troops. The women and others left in the fort had all heard the massive gunfire and feared the worst. Once the troops were through the gates, Carrington announced the deaths of Bowers and Bingham. The gasps from the women were somewhat muted, as neither Bingham nor Bowers had been stationed at the post for a significant period of time and were thus not well known. But it was still a blow to all in the fort.

That evening Grummond, Fetterman, Brown, Captain Tenodor Ten Eyck, and Captain James Powell sat around the bar in Judge Kinney's sutler shop, drinking whiskey and replaying the events of the day.

Grummond was still furious at Carrington. "Goddamn it," he yelled. "When I took off after those savages that old goat should have followed me! Hell, he knows I have seen more damn fighting then he has ever dreamed of. I know what I am doing out there."

Fetterman raised his hand to quiet the brash young lieutenant. "George," he said. "Simmer down now. I agree that Carrington is no fighter. Hell, he came within eyesight of me and my boys fighting it out and he turned away from us. He claims he didn't see or hear us. How do you not hear a battle? That being said, I don't agree with what you did. You disobeyed orders and Carrington could have had you arrested. As well things happened out there faster than I ever saw in the war with the rebels. You can't just go blindly charging into god knows what. I could have lost my command back there and you were very nearly killed. We need to stick together. A soldier is a damn sight better fighter than any of those red bastards. But that won't be enough if they get us outnumbered 100-1 or so. Next time we are out there George, you stick with me or whoever the commanding officer is. Do you hear me?"

Grummond looked at Fetterman sullenly. "I hear you," he muttered. "But I was trying to force those bastards to stand and fight. I think they learned a lesson out there. And that is don't get too close to me and my blade! You should have heard the sound my saber made when it hit red flesh. When it hit the bone it made a 'clicking sound.' I never heard that before. And my god the look on that savages' face when I sliced his arm right off. He didn't know what happened!" Grummond then began almost convulsing in laughter. "It's going to be hard for old Bear Balls, or whatever the fuck his name is to hunt buffalo with only one arm."

Grummond began roaring in laughter again and was joined by Brown and Powell. Powell spit a long stream of tobacco juice on the floor and asked, "Maybe his medicine man can sew it back on", and more laughter went around the room at that thought.

Grummond turned to the very quiet Ten Eyck and asked, "Captain you haven't said much of anything except give me another drink. Why are you so quiet?"

The taciturn officer replied, "Lieutenant, it sounds like you showed a lot of guts today but I really question your brains. Charging ahead with no one to support you, into an opposing force that you knew nothing about. Doesn't sound like a wise move to me. And I have been out here a lot longer than you have and would hope I have learned a thing or two."

Grummond exploded in rage. "You old bastard", he screamed. "What the hell do you know? I am more of a soldier than you could ever hope to be!"

Ten Eyck was an introspective, quiet, well educated, and exceptionally well read gentleman. He was 47 years old and a very talented engineer. His only weakness was he was also an exceptionally heavy drinker. But although drunk he didn't let Grummond's words "set him off."

"Lieutenant," he replied. "If you ever speak to a superior officer like that again I will have you arrested immediately. Your career will be over."

Ten Eyck then pushed his chair back and stood up to leave. "And Lieutenant I really hope you are the soldier that you think you are. Because I have no doubt you are going to throw caution to the wind again, and you will get you and your men into some god-awful mess that only an exceptional soldier with help from god will be able to get out of. Good night gentlemen."

Captain Ten Eyck then took his leave and walked through the bitter cold night air to his quarters.

Fetterman watched the scene with Grummond and Ten Eyck, and felt a weight in his stomach. He admired Grummond's fighting spirit and passion, but Ten Eyck's words made a huge impression on him. He also knew the Sioux and Cheyenne had been almost on top of his command before he knew they were there. He had never seen an ambush happen that fast during the Civil War. He was going to have to rethink his ways of fighting.

That night as the Carringtons lay in bed, Henry turned to his wife and said, "Margaret that young Grummond scares me. I have never seen anyone who is so eager for battle and who absolutely loves to fight. If he wasn't a soldier he'd probably be a murderer. And if I wasn't so short of experienced officers I'd send him home, just to get him out of here. He could have gotten himself and a lot of others killed when he disobeyed me today."

Margaret Carrington looked at her husband and replied, "Henry you need to do what is best. I personally find him quite dashing and his wife Frances is adorable. When we have our parties they are such good company. But if you are worried that he will get others killed maybe you should ask for him to be transferred. "

Henry Carrington looked at the ceiling and said, "No I can't afford to lose him. I'll have to keep him on a tight leash though. Next month after we leave he becomes someone else's problem. "

After leaving the sutler's, George Grummond staggered back to his quarters and crawled into bed with his wife Frances. He was surprised to find her still awake. "Why are you still up," he slurred.

"Why am I still awake," Frances said. "Maybe because you nearly got yourself killed today! George, I heard what you did, galloping off on your own. It sounds as if it was pure luck that you escaped with your life. Haven't you ever thought about what happens to me and your unborn child if you get yourself killed? What would we do without you?"

George Grummond looked at his wife. "Don't you worry my dear. There wasn't a rebel good enough to take me down and there sure isn't any Injun, man enough to take me. We are going to have a long life together."

On December 9, 1866 Lieutenant Bingham and Sergeant Bowers were laid to rest. Lieutenant Bingham had been a Mason and was buried with the full honors accorded that society, with Lieutenant Grummond conducting the rites. When Chaplain White began the religious service for Sergeant Bowers, Captain Fred Brown stepped forward and placed his Army of the Cumberland badge on the dead soldier's chest. Brown, along with Captain Powell and Lieutenant Bisbee, had served in the Civil War with Sergeant Bowers and held him in the highest respect.

After the funeral service, a wagon with Lieutenant Bisbee, his wife and son, along with an escort of nine troopers left the fort on their way to Fort Laramie.

Over the next number of days, the officers worked hard to drill the men. Carrington knew disaster had been narrowly avoided days earlier and he was now ready to pour all the resources necessary into ensuring his troops were ready for the next battle, which he was sure would be soon. Fetterman drilled the infantry relentlessly until they were superbly proficient in firing their muskets by file and by numbers. Powell worked hard with the cavalry on such tactics, as mounting and dismounting, and firing carbines and revolvers while mounted. Grummond was given full command of the mounted infantry and ordered to ensure that all healthy mounts were to be saddled and ready for action 24 hours per day.

That same week, the Carringtons hosted a party at their quarters. Officers appeared in their finest dress uniforms, while the ladies were formally attired in beautiful long dresses. The most popular couple was the Grummonds. Frances, even while pregnant, looked beautiful in her dress, and fairly glowed with the joy of her soon expected child. George Grummond looked and acted as the perfect, chivalrous officer. At one point, Margaret Carrington approached Captain Fetterman and asked, "Captain, forgive me for being so forward but I have heard that perhaps you feel my husband isn't aggressive enough to suit you."

William Fetterman was shocked that she would ask a question such as that. In these Victorian times, ladies didn't usually intrude in their husband's business. However, Fetterman, who was certainly a gentleman, replied, "Mrs. Carrington, I hold your husband in the highest of esteem. Yes, when I was posted here I was concerned that he didn't have the level of combat experience that I have. I certainly respect that he went out on the mission with us on the 6th and he certainly conducted himself quite capably. I don't have much longer to serve with him until he moves onto his next duty assignment and I am positive he will prove to be most capable at that."

Fetterman then nodded his head and said "Mrs. Carrington, I believe I will avail myself of another drink. It was a pleasure speaking with you."

As Fetterman got his fresh drink, George Grummond came over to him. 'What did she want Will," Grummond asked.

"She surprised me. She asked me if I thought the Colonel wasn't aggressive enough. Course I don't think he is but I didn't say that to her. I told her that I was concerned that he didn't have the combat experience I have, but he handled his troops capably on the 6th and I feel he will do very well in his next assignment."

Grummond roared with laughter. "Will that was very elegantly said. Maybe when you retire you can become a diplomat."

While there was great activity within the walls of the fort with the troops drilling, all was quiet outside the walls until Wednesday, December 19th. That morning, Carrington was alerted that the pickets on Signal Hill were warning of an attack on the wood train. As the troops mustered on the parade ground, Carrington placed Captain Powell in charge. His orders were clear; "Heed the lessons of the 6th. Do not pursue Indians across Lodge Trail Ridge." [25]

---

25 Ibid, pg 184.

Captain Powell followed his orders to the letter. He kept his men – especially Lieutenant Grummond, close to him. They relieved the wood train, and as the hostiles saw he wasn't pursuing them they broke off contact and disappeared.

On the evening of December 20th, Carrington was working in his office when Captains Fetterman and Brown arrived. They wanted to discuss a plan they had come up with and were seeking Carrington's approval. Fred Brown explained the plan. "Colonel," he began. "Captain Fetterman and I have spoken to many of the civilians here. We have 50 well-armed civilians who are willing to join a force of 50 mounted troopers on an expedition to clean the Sioux and Cheyenne out of their winter camps along the Tongue River. Sir I urge you to let us try. I know we got a scare two weeks ago. But now we know what to expect. We can't just sit here."

Carrington listened politely and then responded. "Gentlemen the answer is no. I can't spare 100 men for an expedition. That would leave our post almost helpless in case of an attack. If it was a quick strike to drive off another hostile attack I'd consider it. But for an expedition that would take our forces far from the post? The answer is no."

Brown began to argue, but Fetterman placed his hand on his friend's arm. He faced Carrington and said, "Sir, Captain Brown and I understand. We are sorry to have bothered you."

With that, Fetterman and Brown left Carrington's office. Fred Brown looked at his friend and asked, "Will what the hell was that all about? If you had let me push him I think I could have made him change his mind. Goddamn it, I am leaving here next month and before I go I want another crack at those red bastards!"

William Fetterman stared at Brown and replied, "Fred he wasn't going to change his mind. He is weak and I think his little taste of combat two weeks ago scared him. The best we can hope for is the next time the wood cutting party gets hit; I'll lead the relief column and see if at that point I can cut loose from Carrington. Now let's call it a night. "

With that the two officers returned to their respective quarters.

Margaret Carrington came into her husband's office after Fetterman and Brown left. "Henry," she began. What did Captains Fetterman and Brown want?"

Henry Carrington responded, "They wanted permission to lead an expedition of 100 men against the hostiles. They wanted to strike the hostiles right in their camps. I denied them permission as I can't run the risk of sending such a large force so far from the fort. It would leave us dangerously vulnerable to attack. But I have been thinking. Fetterman is my most experienced combat officer. The next time he leads a relief column out in support of the wood cutting party I may 'let him off the leash' just a little. If any man here can defeat the hostiles it is William Fetterman. Maybe if I give him some freedom he can whip the hostiles and they will in return leave us alone. That will get General Cooke off my back as well. I don't know what else to do Margaret. We can't just sit here."

Margaret Carrington looked at her husband. "Henry, I think that sounds very wise. Captain Fetterman certainly has the credentials to defeat the hostiles. From what you told me he handled his troops very effectively two weeks ago. Perhaps if you give him the freedom to act, while he is still in close proximity to the fort that would be a very prudent decision on your part."

"I do believe that is the course of action I will follow. Now I believe it is time we turned in.

ENTERING HELL

Friday, December 21, 1866, was a bitterly cold, sunny day. The officers hurried through reviewing their troops in order to minimize the amount of time the men were standing in the biting cold. The snow was deep on the ground and, to the concern of many, was blowing in huge banks against the outside walls of the stockade. More than one officer muttered under his breath that pretty soon the hostiles would be able to clamber up the snow banks and over the walls of the stockade. A truly terrifying thought!

At 10 am, the wood-train moved out. Carrington, concerned about the safety of the woodcutters, sent a force of 90 heavily armed men to protect them. Just after 11 am, as he worked in his office, Carrington heard the cry of alarm from the sentries; "Pickets report the wood train under attack."

Carrington sprang out of his chair and ran from his office into the bright sunshine. He glanced at Pilot Hill and could see the pickets waving flags indicating the wood-train was under attack. The gunfire from the escorts protecting the wood-train was loud, drawing people throughout the fort outdoors.

Captain Powell ran up to his commanding officer and said, "Sir, the wood-train is under attack."

"I am aware of that. Take command of a detachment, Captain Powell," ordered the colonel, "and drive those hostiles away. You will simply relieve the wood-train. Do not follow the hostiles and invite any unnecessary engagement. Do exactly what you did two days ago."

"Yes sir," Powell responded. He then saluted and ran towards the stables.

As soon as Powell headed towards the stables, Captain William Fetterman approached Colonel Carrington.

"Colonel, I respectfully request command of the relief column sir," Fetterman stated.

"Captain Fetterman, on what basis do you make your request?" Carrington asked. (He in fact knew what answer would be forthcoming.)

"Colonel, you are well aware my brevet rank was Colonel. I thus claim command of the column due to outranking Captain Powell. Sir," Fetterman stated firmly.

Carrington knew that he had no choice here. Fetterman was 100% correct. "Very well Captain, the command of the relief column is yours. But listen closely. You have pushed me to allow you a chance to punish these savages. Now you have your chance. Don't put your command into a situation where you will be heavily outnumbered as I don't have much relief that I can send to you. But if you can hit them - hit them hard. Am I clear?"

Captain William J. Fetterman couldn't believe his ears. His heart skipped a beat. Cowardly old Colonel Henry Carrington was going to turn him loose! He regained his composure, looked at his commanding officer and said, "Your orders are very clear Colonel. I will carry them out. "

"Go get them Captain," Carrington then said.

With that, Captain Fetterman began hurrying to his quarters to retrieve his personal weapons. As he did so, Captain Fred Brown ran up to him. "Will I am coming with you. I still have a score to settle with those red bastards. And I am not leaving around here until I take Red Cloud's scalp."

"Grab your weapons Fred," Fetterman answered. "There are going to be a lot of squaws crying tonight in their teepees as their husbands and sons won't be coming home. Carrington has given me permission to go after them!"

Brown stood there for a moment, "thunderstruck." "Mother, Mary and Joseph, Will, old Henry Carrington has seen the light," Brown then bellowed. "Lucifer better be ready, as there are a lot of red bastards who will be joining him in hell in a very short time from now!"

Brown and Fetterman grabbed their personal weapons and ran back to the parade ground, where bellowing sergeants had the infantry assembled outside of the Company A barracks. Fetterman quickly conducted an inspection and selected 49 soldiers from Companies A, C, and E, whom he felt were ready to march there and then.

In the Grummonds' quarters, a wildly emotional scene was taking place. George Grummond was hurriedly buckling on his saber and holster and preparing to leave. He slid one Remington Army .44 caliber revolver into his holster, and two more into his belt. His revolvers, as all were at the time, were "cap and ball" percussion revolvers. They were very accurate and packed "one hell of a punch," but they took an experienced soldier about six minutes to load, which meant reloading under fire was impossible. (A soldier had to insert gunpowder into each of the six chambers, and then insert a lead ball on top of the powder. Then they used the pistol's ram-rod to ram the ball down into the powder. After that the opening of each chamber would be coated with bear grease to ensure that the blast from the revolver firing one chamber didn't set off the volatile black powder in the other chambers. From there a percussion "cap" had to be placed onto the "nipples" at the back of each chamber. [The chambers on a "cap and ball" were not bored through.]) Thus, a soldier would normally carry two or more into battle, ensuring he had a sizable amount of firepower readily available.

Frances Grummond looked at her husband and cried out, "George don't go. Captain Powell can take the cavalry. He has been training with them more than you. You have your unborn child to think of. Please you were nearly killed two weeks ago. Don't leave me. "

George Grummond stared at his wife. "Darling," he said. "I have to go. I am 100 times the soldier James Powell is. Fetterman needs me with him. And there are a lot of Injuns out there that need killing. I am just the man for that."

With that, Grummond left his quarters and hurried over to Lieutenant Wands, who was serving as Officer of the Day, and sought permission to command the cavalry detachment. Wands ran the request by Carrington, who agreed. Carrington, however, walked over to Grummond and stated that he (Grummond) was to stay with Fetterman and follow his orders to the letter. Grummond nodded his assent. He then conducted a hurried inspection of the cavalry troopers of Company C, and selected 27 soldiers who he felt were prepared to move out immediately. As he did this, Carrington sent Lieutenant Wands over to Grummond to repeat the orders. Again Grummond nodded his head and agreed that he understood them.

As the soldiers prepared to move out, two civilians, James Wheatley and Isaac Fisher, rode up to Fetterman. Both men were holding brand new Henry repeating rifles – the most advanced firearm of the day. The Henry had a 16-shot magazine, allowing it to fire that many rounds before being reloaded. It was a tremendous improvement over the cavalry's seven-shot Starr carbine, and "light years" ahead of the infantry's single-shot, muzzle-loading Springfield muskets.

"Captain Fetterman, sir. Permission to join your column," James Wheatley asked. "Isaac and I served in the War Between the States and have been under fire before. And we are packing," he emphasized as both he and Fisher raised their Henry rifles, ensuring that Fetterman saw them. "And I have a score to settle with those red bastards. They owe me for one good cow."

Fetterman quickly glanced at the two men and said, "Permission granted men. Happy to have you both aboard. You'll ride with Lieutenant Grummond and the cavalry. "

Fetterman then gave the order, and the infantry marched through the front gates. Grummond was still scrambling to get the cavalry organized, and would join Fetterman in short order.

As Grummond began to move out, Carrington mounted the sentry platform and bellowed, "Lieutenant Grummond! Remember, join up with Captain Fetterman and follow his orders implicitly! Do not leave him!"

Grummond nodded his head and waved at his commanding officer, and then gave his horse the spurs. His cavalry detachment raced to catch up to Fetterman's infantry, who were marching double-time. Observers from the fort quickly saw that Fetterman wasn't marching west towards the wood-train as Captain Powell had done two days earlier. Instead his force was marching north-east — almost as if he was maneuvering to cut off the hostiles when they retreated from the wood-train. Captain James Powell seeing this turned to Lieutenant Alexander Wands and said, "Alex, Fetterman isn't going to the wood-train. He must be ignoring Carrington's orders and maneuvering to cut them off. My god, those redskins are going to rue the day that they tangled with William Fetterman if he can catch them."

Captain Ten Eyck seeing the direction Fetterman's column was moving in, immediately rushed to Carrington. "Sir," he began. "Are you aware that Captain Fetterman isn't proceeding towards the wood-train?"

"I am," replied Carrington.

Ten Eyck, then asked, "But Sir, are you not going to recall him? Shall I send an orderly to him and find out what in blazes he is doing?"

Carrington responded carefully. It wouldn't hurt to allow the illusion that Fetterman was striking out on his own. If he was successful then Carrington was happy to see Fetterman win some glory. If he was not, then Carrington could simply argue Fetterman disobeyed his orders.

"No Captain Ten Eyck", he began. "Fetterman obviously has a plan. He is an experienced officer and I will allow him to proceed. If he happens to catch the hostiles then he will have an opportunity to see if he can whip them as he often says he can. If not I'll question him when he returns."

"Very good sir," a surprised Ten Eyck replied. "One thing is for sure. Putting Grummond with Fetterman ensures there will be one hell of a fight today. And I only hope that those two can win it."

Carrington replied, "Captain I am of the same mind as you. May god be with them."

Grummond's cavalry quickly caught up to the swiftly marching infantry. Grummond rode up beside Fetterman who turned to the fiery, young officer and said, "Lieutenant stay close to me. We are going to cut off the hostiles as they withdraw from the wood-train. Don't go off all halfcocked like you did two weeks ago. I need you with me!"

Grummond smiled and responded, "Don't worry Captain Fetterman. I'll be with you and the snow here will run red with Injun blood when we are done with them."

Back at the fort, Carrington spotted a party of perhaps 20 hostiles racing across the top of the bluffs. Seeing as they were within range of his howitzers, he ordered his artillery to open fire. High explosive shells exploded into the hills and the hostiles took off in full retreat, leaving one warrior who had been shredded by shrapnel behind.

Meanwhile, Fetterman had now properly deployed Grummond's cavalry in advance of his infantry and along his flanks. Ahead of his force were a large number of warriors who seemed to slip in and out of rifle range. On several occasions, Fetterman halted his command and ordered his infantry to open fire. His soldiers would kneel down and fire their Springfield muskets. Always the hostiles seemed to be just beyond range, leaving his soldiers frustrated. Fetterman cursed under his breath, "Why in god's name won't they stand and fight us like the infernal rebels would?"

The small party of warriors whom Carrington had fired upon with his artillery came into view and joined up with the others Fetterman was pursuing. Among the Sioux in this group was one of the greatest fighting men in North American history. His name was Crazy Horse and just slightly less than 10 years later he would lead the Sioux and Cheyenne to an overwhelming victory over Lieutenant Colonel George Armstrong Custer's 7th Cavalry at the Battle of Little Big Horn in modern day Montana.

It was now close to noon. "Why won't they stand and fight us?" Grummond raged in frustration as the Sioux and Cheyenne remained just beyond rifle range. Lieutenant George Washington Grummond now looked back at Fetterman's infantry, who were laboring uphill through the snow. He thought to himself; "We'll never catch those red bastards if I have to stay with these foot soldiers."

With that Grummond screamed, "C'mon boys let's get them!" He drove his spurs furiously into the side of his mount and took off at a full gallop.

Sergeant Garrett bellowed, "Follow the Lieutenant boys, let's go!"

Isaac Fisher looked at his friend James Wheatley, and said," Jim, do we follow that fool or stick with Fetterman?"

Wheatley replied, "We'd better go with Grummond. He is going to need us."

Fetterman was horrified at the sight of his cavalry abandoning him. He screamed for Grummond to return and when that didn't work urged his troops to move faster. He looked around and was stunned to see his old friend Captain Fred Brown had also gone with Grummond.

Grummond's cavalry galloped up the west side of Lodge Trail Ridge and down its slope in hot pursuit of Crazy Horse and the other hostiles. As Grummond's troops raced into the gulley at the bottom of the ridge "all hell exploded around them." Crazy Horse gave a signal and over 2,000 Sioux, Cheyenne, and Arapaho who had concealed themselves behind rocks, trees, in the snow and grass, sprang out and filled the air with thousands of arrows.

"Holy shit!" James Wheatley screamed. He and Isaac Fisher dove from their mounts and headed for nearby rocks that could provide them with some cover. They didn't attempt to flee, as they knew that running from Indians was practically suicide. Their only hope was to fight and hope for the best.

Fred Brown, who had been lagging behind the rest of the cavalry, instantly swung his horse about and rammed his spurs into the side of his mount. He knew running from Indians rarely was successful, but he could immediately see that standing and fighting in this case meant certain death. He drew his revolver, leaned low over his horse's neck, and snapped off several shots while galloping back towards Fetterman.

Grummond meanwhile reacted instantly. "Dismount! Fight on foot!" he bellowed. "Form a skirmish line!"

His stunned cavalry troopers leaped off their horses and attempted to form a skirmish line as arrows descended on them like a rain of death. The horse-holders were unable to control their terrified mounts, and the horses broke free and fled the battlefield. The troopers kneeled down and began firing into the multitudes of warriors who were swarming in on their flanks. Soldiers were already keeling over with arrows protruding from their bodies. Massed warriors charged the kneeling cavalry troopers, swinging wooden clubs studded with nails and tomahawks.

Grummond, cackling wildly, waded right into the charging hostiles, and began swinging his saber. "C'mon and get it you bastards," he yelled. "I'll send you all to hell!" he shrieked as he slashed widely with the razor sharp blade. The first Sioux who came close to the enraged lieutenant was instantly decapitated. The head flew off his body, landing about 5 yards from where the warrior's body crumbled. Grummond then disemboweled an Arapaho who had charged him waving a war club. The warrior fell to his knees and stared in horror as his intestines flowed out of the massive wound in his abdomen. The snow around the disemboweled Arapaho quickly became bright red. Another Sioux charged Grummond, who plunged his saber into his chest. The blade became stuck in the Sioux and Grummond couldn't yank it out. He let it go and drew the 44 caliber Remington revolver that was in his holster. Lieutenant Grummond fired point blank into an on-rushing Cheyenne's face, blowing the enemy's skull apart. He then fell back into the group of encircled cavalry troopers, emptying that Remington as he did so, and ordered his men to fall back. When his revolver was empty he threw it aside, reached into his belt, and drew another one.

Wheatley and Fisher reached the group of rocks they had spotted, and dove behind them. Isaac Fisher unlimbered his Henry rifle and yelled, "Jim, we have to cover those boys so they have a chance to get back to Fetterman!"

With that the two tough frontiersmen kneeled back to back and "unleashed hell" with their Henry's. The Plains Indians had rarely come across repeating rifles before; they were stunned at the massive, unending barrage of deadly accurate fire coming from Wheatley and Fisher. Sergeant Garrett and two other cavalry troopers dove behind the rocks and joined Wheatley and Fisher. The tough civilians pumped the levers time and time again on their Henry rifles, and grimly poured fire into the masses of enraged Sioux, Cheyenne, and Arapaho. The three soldiers added fire from their Spencer carbines (Carrington had stripped the regimental band of their modern Spencer's and had distributed the weapons amongst the cavalry.)

"Welcome to hell boys!" James Wheatley yelled as the soldiers arrived. "The only way we are getting out of here is to keep up this fire until Fetterman can get here and haul our asses out of here."

Sergeant Garrett roared as he began blasting away with his Spencer carbine, "Mother of all fucking god! Where did all these redskins come from? What the hell have we gotten into?"

The massed warriors now fell back from the devastating fire coming from the civilians and now augmented by the three soldiers joining them. The ground in front of their position was covered in the corpses of dead warriors. The thunder of the Henry rifles, along with the "sharp bark" of the troopers' Spencer carbines, echoed across the entire battlefield, drowning out the screams of agony of the wounded and dying and war whoops from the Indians.

With the overwhelming cover fire coming from the Wheatley-Fisher position, the surviving cavalry troopers began a slow retreat on foot back towards Fetterman. The young soldiers, with their sergeants and Grummond trying desperately to keep them under some control, fired their seven-shot Starr and Spencer carbines and six-shot revolvers as they slowly retreated back up the slope.

Fetterman, already rushing to catch up with Grummond, heard the massive crash of gunfire and thought; "Holy shit Grummond is really into it now."

As he reached the crest of the hill, Captain Brown, who had escaped the trap that had ensnared Grummond and his cavalry, raced up the slope and joined with Fetterman. "Will;" he screamed. "Jesus Christ, the whole Sioux nation is down there. They are cutting Grummond and his boys to pieces!"

Fetterman could hear the thunderous barrage of gunfire and see the swarming warriors attacking the dismounted cavalry troopers and the Wheatley-Fisher position. He had two choices. He could retreat and attempt to reach the safety of the fort, leaving the cavalry to their fate. Or he could advance with his force of young, still fairly raw troops with their obsolete Springfield muskets and attempt to rescue Grummond's shattered command. Fetterman made his decision very quickly.

"Fred!" he yelled. "Stick with me. We are going in there and we are going to haul Grummond's ass out of there." He then turned to his troops." Men!" he yelled. "The cavalry has got themselves in a real pickle down there. American soldiers never abandon their comrades. We are going in there and we are rescuing our friends. Fix bayonets men and let's move out!"

The infantry drew the razor sharp bayonet blades from their belts and slammed them into the holders on the muzzle of their Springfields. They then began their advance into what appeared to be "hell on earth." One young soldier in Fetterman's command looked at the soldier beside him and with a simply terrified look on his face muttered, "John you had better start praying and praying right now.

We are in for some serious shit down there."

Back at Fort Phil Kearny, "time now seemed to stand still." Everyone in the fort heard the explosion of gunfire when Grummond's cavalry was ambushed, and they stepped out of their quarters and gathered. Nobody could see the action from the fort but from the sustained massive firing that continued, it was apparent to all, that the battle Fetterman, Brown and Grummond had craved had finally occurred. People turned to the person next to them, and asked their opinion on what was occurring. The general consensus was that Fetterman was whipping the hostiles.

Frances Grummond turned away from the other women she was with to hurry back to her quarters. She listened to the explosions of gunshots and feared for the life of her husband. She knew he would not be in the rear of any action – he would be in the forefront. The question in her mind now was she going to be a widow at the end of the day or the wife of a military hero.

Colonel Carrington, hearing the firing and fearing the worst, summoned Captain Ten Eyck. He didn't feel as confident as many others did in the fort.

"Captain Ten Eyck," Carrington began. "Fetterman is engaged and I believe he will need support. Gather a relief column as quickly as possible and proceed immediately to his aid. You are to render onto him whatever aid his forces require."

Captain Ten Eyck snapped a sharp salute and replied, "Very good sir. I will gather the men and proceed forthwith to Captain Fetterman's assistance."

Carrington and Ten Eyck were then interrupted by shouts from the sentries. "Horses approaching!" the sentries cried.

Carrington and Ten Eyck ran to the sentry platform and quickly mounted it. What they saw made their blood run cold. A herd of US Army cavalry horses was galloping towards the fort. However, there were no soldiers mounted on them. In a split-second both officers knew something terrible had happened to Grummond and his command.

Margaret Carrington had joined her spouse and Ten Eyck on the sentry platform. "Dear," she said to her husband. "Do you think it is as bad as it looks? It can't be good if there are no men coming back with their horses."

Colonel Carrington looking positively ashen glanced at his wife and responded, "Darling, I fear that Lieutenant Grummond has gotten embroiled in a situation that he may not be able to get out of."

Meanwhile Grummond's shattered command was now cut off about a quarter mile from the Wheatley-Fisher position. They had attempted to withdraw up the snow covered hill, boots slipping on the icy surface, while also attempting to keep up a heavy covering fire. Their retreat up the slope however had now been cut off. They were completely encircled. Grummond had his men kneel in a circle and begin pouring volleys of fire into enemy.

"Keep firing men!" he roared. "Hang on, Fetterman is coming!" He then turned to his bugler Adolph Metzger and screamed, "Trumpeter! Blow recall! Blow damn it blow! Fetterman needs to know that we need his help!"

The sharp notes of Metzger's bugle now echoed through the hills. It was a final, desperate cry for help from a small group of brave men who knew their time on earth was rapidly coming to an end if help didn't arrive quickly. Grummond's second revolver clicked on an empty chamber and he tossed it aside. He then reached into his belt and drew his third and final revolver.

Fetterman had his infantry now advancing down the slope towards the cut off cavalry troopers. He heard the bugle and urged his men to move faster. He knew Grummond was in desperate trouble. Already some of Fetterman's men were dropping from arrows slamming into them. Many warriors who had encircled the cavalry now charged towards the slow-moving infantry, who were marching right into the ambush that they had sprung.

There were now three separate engagements raging. Wheatley and Fisher, along with the three cavalry troopers, were holding their own for the moment. Grummond's cavalry troopers were fighting for their lives, and Fetterman was closing in with his infantry.

Arrows were slamming into the cavalry troopers decimating their ranks. Grummond had just emptied his final revolver when a Sioux arrow buried itself in his neck. A deluge of blood exploded from the young lieutenant's mouth and poured down the front of his jacket. He gasped, dropped to his knees and then fell over dead.

With their commanding officer dead, the remaining cavalry troopers broke ranks and made a run for it, trying desperately to reach Fetterman. Very few made it. Most were cut down before they could reach the "safety" that Fetterman represented. One of the last cavalry troopers to die was bugler Adolph Metzger. He emptied his Spencer carbine then drew his revolver and rapidly emptied that. As Sioux and Cheyenne warriors then charged him, he met them swinging his bugle and cussing them in German. He was dispatched by a war club blow to the head that crushed his skull.

Meanwhile, Isaac Fisher and James Wheatley, along with the three cavalry troopers, kept up their barrage of fire. They had done their best to cover Grummond's retreat, and were now fighting for their own lives. The Sioux, Cheyenne, and Arapaho were desperate to close in and destroy their tormentors. The firepower emanating from here had simply wreaked havoc amongst the massed warriors.

Fisher turned to Wheatley as he cranked the lever of his Henry and sent another deadly round into the mass of hostiles and asked, "Jim do you think Grummond got his men out of here?"

James Wheatley responded, "I don't know. I can't see anything with all this smoke. Just keep firing. Fetterman will hear us and get us out of here."

Just then, the first trooper in the little redoubt went down with a Cheyenne arrow buried in his neck. Shortly after that, Sergeant Garrett keeled over with an arrow embedded in his heart. Moments later Isaac Fisher gasped, "Jim I am hit."

Wheatley turned away from his targets that were closing in, and saw his friend with an arrow protruding from his back. He obviously had a pierced lung, as bloody bubbles and gurgling sounds sprayed from his mouth. Fisher lay thrashing on the ground in obvious death throes.

"Christ in heaven Isaac!" James Wheatley exclaimed.

With the sudden decrease in fire coming from the position the hostiles charged. James Wheatley turned away from his dying friend, pumped another round into an on-rushing enemy, blowing the warrior backwards with a massive, gaping wound in his chest, and then leapt up to meet the onslaught. He shattered the stock of his Henry rifle across a Cheyenne skull. Then, as he attempted to pull his Bowie knife, gasped at the appearance of a tip of a spear protruding from his own chest. A Sioux had run him through from behind. Wheatley dropped to his knees, another Sioux caved in his skull with a nail studded war club, and he rolled over dead.

With the cavalry and the Wheatley-Fisher position now fallen, the over 2,000 enraged warriors charged towards Fetterman and his young, poorly armed infantry. Fetterman spotted a formation of large boulders. He realized the only hope for his men was to fall back there, make a stand and wait for Carrington to rush help to him. He roared, "Fall back to the rocks, on the double!"

With the assistance of Fred Brown, the soldiers made a run for the rocks. They reached their objective, and Fetterman and Brown frantically organized them into a circular defensive formation and then began a slow, steady fire. All the drilling that Fetterman had put the infantry through was now paying off as his young soldiers began their defensive fire. They staggered their shots so that there was always some fire being directed at the rapidly advancing enemy.

Fred Brown bellowed; "Men, remember what Captain Fetterman has been teaching you! Slow and steady fire. Keep it up!"

The first two volleys of musket fire cut down charging warriors like wheat before a scythe. The problem the troops faced was that their weapons were simply so poor. A well-trained veteran soldier could fire between two to possibly three shots per minute with the Springfield musket. Against a rapidly advancing enemy who outnumbered them better than 20-1 that simply wasn't good enough. And add to that a musket cannot be fired in anything but a standing position. Which meant a soldier reloading a musket was a prime target with no cover.

Back at Fort Phil Kearny, Captain Ten Eyck had by now gathered a force of 40 mainly infantry troops, led them through the gates of the fort, and was advancing towards the firing in the distance. As he was doing so, Carrington was frantically trying to gather additional troops to support Ten Eyck. The issue as always was working weapons. So many of the soldiers' muskets were barely functional, if they worked at all.

When they reached Big Piney Creek, the soldiers quickly pulled off their boots and stockings and rushed through the icy water, putting them back on after they crossed. As the troops got across the creek the sound of firing was ominously slowing down.

Lieutenant Winfield Scott Matson turned to Captain Ten Eyck and asked, "Sir there isn't as much shooting now. What do you think that means?"

Ten Eyck looked grimly at Matson. "Lieutenant, either Fetterman has pulled back or he is losing this fight. And I fear the worst. I think Grummond got them into a mess that it will take God himself to rescue them from."

A short marching distance away, the end was near for Captain William Fetterman and his men. They simply could not keep up a sustained fire with their obsolete weapons. As his men struggled to reload, the hostiles made a massed charge on Fetterman's position. Seeing what appeared to be death closing in, Fetterman screamed, "Men prepare to fight with bayonets!"

Brown turned to his friend Fetterman and said, "Will, this is it! God bless you and we'll see each other in a better place."

After screaming the order, Fetterman and Brown stood side by side at the forefront of their troops, and emptied their revolvers into the onrushing mass of warriors. The hostiles slammed into Fetterman's group of young soldiers. The soldiers rammed their bayonets into their attackers. Numerous warriors staggered back with a razor-sharp bayonet blade buried in their guts. Other warriors swung axes, clubs studded with nails, and tomahawks, crushing and shattering white skulls. The soldiers, in desperation, swung their muskets as clubs, and drew knives and revolvers. Savage, bloody, hand-to-hand combat exploded. No mercy was expected and none was given. The fighting was ferocious. After emptying his revolver Fetterman drew his saber and began slashing at every non-white body within his circle of reach. His ferocious counterattack left horribly slashed and mutilated native corpses littering the terrain.

Despite the spirited and desperate resistance of the soldiers, the sheer mass of the equally courageous and furious Sioux, Cheyenne and Arapaho warriors began to roll over the outnumbered troops. Fetterman retreated to the rear, slashing and stabbing with his saber until it became imbedded into a Cheyenne warrior and he was unable to draw it out.

Seeing the mass of warriors swarming over the badly outnumbered soldiers, Captain Fred Brown, retreating to the rear, remembered the old saying that veterans on the frontier always said; "Keep the last bullet for yourself." The thought of being captured alive, and a slow death by torture, wasn't something anyone wished to face. Brown drew his final revolver, fired the first five shots into the mass of hostiles in front of him, and then before a Sioux or Cheyenne could "take him out" put his pistol to his temple and blew his own brains out.

Fetterman watched in horror as his old friend committed suicide. As his forces disintegrated, he frantically drew and rapidly emptied a final revolver. As he did so, a young soldier who had lost his musket ran to him and screamed, "Captain please save me! Oh god, I am only 19! I don't want to die!"

As he finished those last words, he then fell to his knees crying and buried his head into his hands. A Cheyenne warrior rushed forwards and crushed his skull with a massive nail studded club. The soldier's head exploded in a mass of blood and brains.

Fetterman dropped his empty revolver and turned to run. He had no more weapons to resist with. Sioux warrior American Horse charged him and swung his war axe viciously. The blade caught Fetterman in the chest, opening a massive fatal wound. Fetterman watched the enormous geyser of blood and internal organs explode from his body. He then rolled over and took his last breath.

There were still a few standouts amongst the infantry that the Sioux and their allies needed to finish off. Within minutes though, the gunfire had ended. For a few moments the Sioux, Cheyenne, and Arapaho viewed the awful carnage. Corpses seemed to be everywhere. Fetterman's infantry were basically piled in one position where they fought and died together. Numerous dead warriors had joined them with either musket balls buried in their bodies (from before the hand-to-hand fighting erupted) or bayonet blades still protruding. Grummond's cavalry lay dead, starting from where the ambush erupted, with corpses strewn up the slope where they had retreated and finally died before reaching Fetterman. And then there was the Wheatley/Fisher position. The two civilians and three soldiers lay dead behind their temporary rock fortress. As Crazy Horse walked around the area, he was stunned at the sheer immense number of dead Indians surrounding the position. The five white men had sold their lives dearly. In particular the rapid and heavy firepower of Wheatley and Fishers' Henry Rifles had killed close to 50 warriors, if not more.

Warriors now moved amongst the dead, stripping them of weapons and anything else of value. As the bodies were looted, the now common mutilations began. Abdomens were cut open and organs ripped out. Eyes were gauged out, scalps taken, and genitals sliced off and then usually stuffed in the dead soldiers' mouth.

The Sioux, Cheyenne, and Arapaho took particular "revenge" on the corpses of James Wheatley and Isaac Fisher. Normally the warriors would respect an enemy who fought and died bravely, and Fisher and Wheatley had certainly done that. However they had killed so many that the respect they held for a brave enemy was overpowered by their hatred for the whites. The warriors crushed the civilians' skulls into "jelly" and hacked their limbs and genitals off.

One body that was left "intact" (or as intact as a body that died in combat can be) was that of Adolph Metzger. The hostiles respected the manner in which the small German bugler had fought and died. His body was left face up and covered with a blanket showing the respect the Indians had for him. Years later, his bugle that had been dented beyond almost any recognition in the final flurry of hand to hand combat, was returned to the army.

As the warriors were finishing their grisly work, the word came back that more troops were advancing towards them rapidly. As this occurred, Captain Ten Eyck's small relief force reached the summit and stared in horror at the scene below. The valley was swarming with what seemed to be thousands of enraged warriors. There was no longer any gunfire nor any signs of Fetterman's command. There did not appear to be any soldiers left who could be rescued by Ten Eyck's force. Hundreds of mounted warriors galloped to the base of the ridge and taunted the soldiers, daring them to come down. Ten Eyck had the reputation of being a cautious (not cowardly – an intelligent and cautious) officer. He wasn't about to sacrifice his command here on a whim.

Ten Eyck roared, "Hold your positions men."

He then ordered one of his few mounted troopers, Private Archibald Sample to ride back to the fort and inform Carrington that, "Captain Ten Eyck says he can see or hear nothing of Captain Fetterman. The Indians are on the road challenging him to come down."

Sample galloped off racing back to Fort Phil Kearny. Meanwhile, an additional 40 soldiers plus a surgeon and hospital wagon had left the fort and were on their way to join Ten Eyck.

Sample reached the fort and saw the wives of Fetterman's men gathered near Carrington's headquarters, grimly watching the hills to the northwest. The gunfire had ended. Now the question was why? Had Fetterman's command emerged victorious? Or had something too horrible to imagine occurred? Frances Grummond, who had joined the other wives in the quarters of Lieutenant Wands, wrote in her diary "the silence was dreadful." [26]

Sample rode up to Carrington, who had stepped out of his office. He provided Carrington with Ten Eyck's message, adding that Ten Eyck was requesting more troops plus one of the howitzers. He also added "the Captain is afraid Fetterman's party is all gone up, sir."

Carrington reeled in shock. His greatest, most horrific nightmare seemed to be coming true. He scribbled a quick order that read:

Captain: Forty well-armed men, with 3,000 rounds, ambulance, etc., left before your courier came in.

You must unite with Fetterman, fire slowly, and keep men in hand; you could have saved two miles toward the scene of action if you had taken Lodge Trail Ridge.

I ordered the wood train in, which will give 50 more men to spare.

H.B Carrington

Colonel Commanding

Carrington would later state he didn't mention the howitzer as he had no fit horses that could pull it.

Sample mounted a fresh horse and galloped back towards Ten Eyck with Carrington's orders in hand. He reached the Captain just after the reinforcements had arrived. As Ten Eyck contemplated his next move the warriors who had been taunting him began pulling back in retreat. Suddenly an enlisted man in his command cried out:

---

[26] Ibid, pg 202

"There're the men down there, all dead!" [27]

Ten Eyck grimly ordered his small force to advance. The scene they discovered was ghastly. Fetterman's infantry lay in a diameter of no more than forty feet. The bodies were beginning to freeze solid, had been stripped and horribly mutilated. Captain Brown was found face down, scalped with a bullet hole through his left temple. Fetterman was also found face down, scalped with a horrific chest wound. A single living member of Fetterman's command was discovered. It was a grey cavalry mount named Dapple Dave who was suffering from over a dozen arrow wounds. Ten Eyck ordered a soldier to put the poor beast out of its misery.

The bodies of Fetterman, Brown, and the infantry were piled into the ambulance wagon. By now it was getting dark and it was again threatening to snow. Captain Ten Eyck reluctantly gave the order to leave the bodies of the fallen cavalry and began the slow journey back to Fort Phil Kearny.

It was a hushed group that met Ten Eyck's command when they passed back through the gates. The scene inside the hospital wagon that they saw was something straight out of Hades. Frank Fessenden, a member of the regimental band, described it as "arms and legs in all shapes, divulging the horrible manner in which our brave comrades had died. It was a horrible and sickening sight, and brought tears to every eye, to see those men, many of whom had served four years in the War of the Rebellion, meeting such an awful death on the western plains." [28]

After Captain Ten Eyck had reported his finding to Carrington, the

---

27 Ibid, pg. 203

28 Ibid, pg 207

shattered colonel collapsed into his office chair. He now knew his fort was in mortal danger. The "cream" of his combat troops had been destroyed, and now there was very serious concern that an "all-out" assault by the hostiles on the fort could be successful.

Margaret Carrington came into her husband's office. He glanced up at her with eyes that were almost vacant. She had never seen such a defeated, almost stunned look on his face. He looked as if he was about to be physically ill.

"Henry," she began. "Is it as bad as I fear it appears?"

"It's worse", he replied. "It doesn't appear that there are any survivors. I simply cannot imagine how an officer as experienced and brave as Fetterman was, could be overwhelmed the way it appears he was. And yet, there is no evidence to be found that any of his men survived. Captain Ten Eyck was only able to bring in the dead infantry. Maybe some of the cavalry were able to escape. I doubt it, as surely they would have made their way back here if they did. But maybe there is some hope. I suppose someone has to go talk to Mrs. Grummond and the other wives of the missing. I'll of course have to speak to the wives we know whose husbands are dead."

"I'll speak with Frances Grummond, Henry. This type of news is better coming from another woman."

With that Margaret Carrington put her coat on and made a slow, sad walk to the quarters of Lieutenant Wands and his wife. When she arrived, she went to Frances Grummond and asked to speak to her privately. When they were alone, Margaret looked at the trembling young woman before her and said: "My dear I am so sorry to have to tell you this. Your gallant husband has not been found alive. Nor was his body recovered. We believe he has been lost along with all of his brave men."

"Is there no hope at all"? Frances Grummond asked in a trembling voice.

"Until we either find his body or he rides into the fort I suppose there is some hope." Margaret Carrington responded. "But be reasonable dear. Even if he somehow escaped those awful Indians, it is well below zero outside. It would take a miracle not to freeze to death. Now you are coming to our quarters and staying with Henry and myself. You are not going to be alone."

Frances Grummond numbly nodded her head. She knew in her heart that her husband was dead. George Grummond was not someone who would flee a battlefield. She knew he would have been in the "heart" of the battle and the fact that he had not yet been found alive was confirmation that he wouldn't be.

She returned to her quarters to gather some personal items, and while there she received a visitor. His name was John (Portugee) Philips. He had arrived at Fort Phil Kearny with Isaac Fisher and James Wheatley, and had accepted employment working for quartermaster Captain Fred Brown. If he had not been hauling water for the post's water barrels he, in all likelihood, would have joined his friends Wheatley and Fisher in volunteering to join Fetterman's ill-fated command. Mrs. Grummond had seen Philips at the fort but had never spoken to him. She was quite surprised at his appearance at her door.

"Mrs. Grummond," he began. "I was a great admirer of your husband. I want you to know that I will ensure you and your unborn child will be safe. I am going to Colonel Carrington after I leave you and am going to offer to ride to Fort Laramie and bring back help."

After a few more words, Philips departed, and then presented himself at the quarters of Colonel Carrington. Carrington met him at the door and said, "Mr. Philips what is it? I am rather busy as you can imagine. We have to prepare the post for an attack that I believe will occur just after nightfall."

Philips responded, "Colonel Carrington, sir. I am well aware of our dire situation. I am also aware that we need reinforcements and quickly. I am offering to ride to Fort Laramie and bring back help."

Carrington looked shocked. It may have been the bravest thing he had ever heard. The odds of Philips surviving such at attempt were astronomical. And yet it had to be tried.

"Mr. Philips I accept your offer although I do so with a heavy heart. You realize that your chances of reaching Fort Laramie are not good, don't you?"

"I know what my chances are Colonel," Philips replied. "I am also well aware that your chances here are very slim if you don't get some reinforcements. I know the area well and I believe I can get through riding at night and hiding during the day."

"Very well, Mr. Philips," Carrington responded. "I will give you my best horse and you will depart tonight. Go make what preparations you believe you must. I want you on the road by 9:pm."

Philips politely nodded and took his leave to get ready. He could see furious activity on the parade grounds as soldiers began to prepare for the attack they felt was imminent. Carrington ordered all doors and windows to be "barred." All men were put on sentry duty, including soldiers locked in the guardhouse for disciplinary infractions. Howitzers were loaded with grape-shot and case-shot and positioned for combat. [29] If the hostiles tried climbing the snow

---

[29] Grape and case-shot are masses of metal balls or slugs enclosed in canvas bags (grape) or brass containers. When fired from a cannon, the canvas bags or brass containers would blow open and the metal balls/slugs would spread

banks piled against the stockade walls, and scaled the walls, the howitzers would decimate them. If they got past that, Carrington had ordered a barricade of wagons to be created in front of the powder magazine. [30]

Carrington then gave grim orders to adjutant Captain Wilbur Arnold, Captain Ten Eyck, Captain Powell, and Lieutenant Wands. Jim Bridger was also present.

"Gentlemen," Carrington began. "Our situation is grim. I am sending John Philips, one of our civilians out tonight to ride to Fort Laramie and return with assistance. I may send another rider out as well. Even if one or both are successful in reaching Fort Laramie it will be at least a week until help arrives. I want every man available under arms. If the hostiles attack, the women and children are to be moved to the powder magazine. We are to hold off the hostiles before they breach the walls. If they do breach the walls the men will fall back to the wagon barricade in front of the powder magazine. They are to make a final stand there. If then it is believed that the position will fall, either myself or the surviving senior officer will enter the powder magazine and ignite it. We cannot allow the women and children to fall into the hands of those heathen savages. Am I clear?"

"Very clear Sir," Lieutenant Wands replied. "We'll pray to god that we don't come to that. If however all else fails we will not allow the women and children to have a fate worse than death, befall them."

---

out and tear into enemy troops very much like a large shotgun. The effect of these weapons on advancing troops was simply devastating.

30 The powder magazine was a large hole in the ground, supported by heavy timbers and covered with earth. It contained all the reserve ammunition for the fort.

Jim Bridger listened calmly to the officers and then added his own thoughts.

"Gentlemen, there is no chance in hell of the Sioux attacking the fort tonight" he began. "They will remain in their villages doing the scalp dance and celebrating their victory over us. We won't see any action tonight. Trust me, I know them."

Carrington listened and then responded.

"Mr. Bridger, not to impugn your knowledge of the enemy. Your opinion is duly noted but I cannot risk the lives of everyone here due to one man's opinion. We will proceed in the manner that I have already described."

Shortly after 9:pm John Philips and another civilian, William Bailey, slipped out the rear gate of the fort and began their desperate trek to Fort Laramie. It would be a ride of over 200 miles, through brutal, subzero winter temperatures, and dodging vigilant Sioux and Cheyenne warriors all the way.

That night, heavily armed men patrolled the grounds of the fort. They mounted the sentry platforms and peered through the darkness and blowing snow desperate to see any sign of impending attack.

The attack didn't come. In fact, Jim Bridger was 100% correct. The hostiles had no intention of mounting such an assault. Not only were they celebrating their victory, they were also mourning their dead. Their casualties had been terrible. They had defeated Fetterman to be sure, but they had paid a horrific price in doing so. North American Plains Indian culture was not a culture that embraced "martyrdom" or anything of that sort. They tried to minimize casualties when possible. When troops would attack a village, the warriors would come out and engage the soldiers just long enough for the village to escape. Then the warriors would pull back. Warriors would make quick "hit and run" attacks on the sentries outside of an army camp.

But they wouldn't attack the camp itself, as they knew if they did so; the massed firepower the troops could bring into action would decimate their ranks. Now they had taken a bold new step, successfully ambushing and engaging a large group of soldiers. They had won, but had suffered the worst casualties they could imagine. [31] It was plain for them to imagine that if they had launched an "all-out assault" on Fort Phil Kearny they may well capture the fort. But the casualties they would suffer doing so would be too terrible to comprehend.

On the morning of December 22, 1866 Colonel Carrington, who hadn't slept "a wink" the night before, gathered the surviving officers in his office. He announced that at the morning roll call Lieutenant Grummond was still reported as missing, along with his men, and in his opinion an expedition must be mounted to recover their bodies. Captains Arnold, Powell, and Ten Eyck, along with Lieutenants Matson and Wands argued against such an action. The consensus was sending out the few remaining troops that they had to retrieve dead bodies was senseless.

Ten Eyck argued "Colonel they are beyond any mortal help. We barely have enough troops left to hold the fort. As much as it pains me to leave our brave comrades out there, it doesn't make sense to risk those few troops we have left to retrieve corpses."

Carrington patiently listened to his officers and then announced his decision.

"I will not let the Indians entertain the conviction that the dead cannot and will not be rescued. If we cannot rescue our dead, as the

---

31 Many Indian and white historians estimate more Indians were killed during the Fetterman battle then were killed during "Custer's Last Stand" at the Little Big Horn in June 1876.

Indians always do at whatever risk, how can you send details out for any purpose, and that single fact would give them an idea of weakness here, and would only stimulate them to risk an assault." [32]

Carrington then announced he would personally lead the expedition of 80 handpicked men, and Captain Ten Eyck and Lieutenant Matson would join him. He then turned to the door leading into an adjoining room and knocked. Margaret Carrington was in the room with Frances Grummond, and Margaret called out to enter. Frances Grummond described what occurred next:

"Mrs. Carrington was sitting near the window deep in thought…I was lying down equally absorbed by the momentous question at stake…When the door opened, we sprang trembling to our feet. The Colonel advanced to his wife and quietly announced his decision…

Turning to me he said 'Mrs. Grummond, I shall go in person, and will bring back to you the remains of your husband.'" [33]

Carrington then returned to his office and wrote out two orders for Captain Powell, who was officer of the day, and thus would be in charge of the fort while Carrington was out retrieving the bodies. The first order involved communications between the fort and Carrington's column. The second was a specific order to Powell that if the Indians attacked while Carrington was out he was to immediately place the women and children in the powder magazine. And if the fort appeared to be about to fall, Powell was to blow the magazine up with everyone in it.

Carrington then led his force out of Fort Phil Kearny and on their grim mission. Jim Bridger, despite suffering from severe arthritis that

---

32 Brown, Dee "The Fetterman Massacre, pgs 212-213.

33 Ibid, pg 213

was aggravated by the cold, supervised a line of pickets that were posted between the fort and the battlefield. Working in brutal, sub zero temperatures, Carrington's men gathered the bodies of their dead comrades. What made their already dismal duty even more terrible was that the bodies, having lain out in below-zero temperatures all night, were frozen solid. Many of their limbs were frozen in unnatural positions. As the bodies were being loaded into the ambulance wagons, many of the frozen limbs had to be broken by their horrified comrades just so all of them could fit in the wagon. All the while, the pickets intently peered into the surrounding hills, looking for any sign that the hostiles would return.

Finn Burnet, one of the civilian volunteers on this most awful mission, later wrote: "It was terrible work to load the frozen corpses into the wagons. The ground was fairly sodden with blood, the smell of which frightened the mules until they were well-nigh unmanageable. A man was obliged to hold the head of every animal while other teamsters loaded the naked, mutilated remains like cordwood into the wagon-boxes." [34]

John Guthrie, a veteran cavalry trooper who was fortunate not have joined Grummond's command the day before, wrote: " Some had crosses cut into their breasts, faces to the sky, some crosses on their backs, faces to the ground, a mark cut that we could not find out. We walked on top of their internals and did not know it in the high grass. Picked them up, that is their internals, did not know what soldiers they belonged to, so you see the cavalryman got an infantryman's guts…"[35]

Lieutenant Grummond's body was found with his head almost

---

34 Ibid, pg 214.

35 Ibid, pgs 214-215.

severed, his fingers chopped off and his body filled with arrows. The scene at the Wheatley-Fisher position stopped everyone "in their tracks." Both Wheatley and Fisher had been killed and scalped. James Wheatley's body had 105 arrows in it. However, the corpses were surrounded by a "mountain" of spent Henry cartridges. In front of their position was a massive ring of dead Indian ponies and at least 65 separate blood trails. It was evident to all that James Wheatley and Isaac Fisher, along with the three cavalry troopers, had put up a tremendous battle and had sold their lives dearly.

Eventually all the bodies were recovered and loaded into wagons, and the column returned to the fort. The first thing Colonel Carrington did when he entered the fort was to see Frances Grummond. He stood before her, his clothing and beard caked in ice, his eyes looking virtually dead.

"Mrs. Grummond," he began. "I have the most solemn duty to inform you that we have found and recovered the body of your most gallant husband. It was clear by the evidence that he died in the manner befitting a brave soldier and you can be proud of that. I have this for you."

He then handed her an envelope and took his leave to give her some privacy in this time of grief. She opened the envelope with trembling hands and found inside it a lock of her husband's hair. Frances Grummond then buried her face into her hands and sobbed uncontrollably. Her whole world, as she saw it, had come to a swift and cruel end. Margaret Carrington then came into the room to attempt to console her. Frances Grummond turned to her and asked: "Mrs. Carrington, what will become of me? I will soon have a child and no husband to take care of us. What will I do? Will I ever get out of this most terrible place?"

Margaret Carrington looked sadly at the devastated young woman. "My dear," she began. "You will receive a pension from the army.

They won't cast you aside. You are educated. You could teach school or something such as that. You have told me you have family. They will help you and your child. As for here, Henry has received new orders. When he leaves next month you will come with us. We will assist you in returning back to your family in Tennessee."

Henry Carrington made the same visit to Jennifer Wheatley, the 19-year old wife of James Wheatley. He formally explained to her that her spouse's body had been recovered, and as he did with Frances Grummond, Carrington explained to Mrs. Wheatley how bravely her husband had fought and died.

"Mrs. Wheatley, I know this is little consolation for you at this time. We have recovered your husband's body. I strongly urge you not to attempt to view it. However I can assure you that he died in the most gallant manner. The evidence of that is beyond question."

As night fell, a massive blizzard began to rage. The temperature plummeted to minus 20 degrees F. Soldiers on guard duty were issued mittens that were almost the length of their arms and leggings that came to their thighs. Boots made of buffalo fur and various fur hats were added. Even with those protective measures, the guards could only work in 30 minute shifts; otherwise, they would risk freezing to death. By the morning of December 23rd, the snow was so deep that guards could walk across the parade ground and over the western wall of the stockade. Carrington ordered a ten-foot trench dug around the outer stockade walls for added security. Attempting to dig into the frozen ground was an almost impossible task, and as they did so the blowing snow filled in the trench faster then they could dig it.

As the guards watched through the snow-filled night, preparations were made to bury the dead. Arrows were either drawn or cut out of bodies. Internal organs when possible were pushed back into the corpses. Most of the dead had been stripped naked by the hostiles so soldiers in the fort volunteered many of their own pieces of uniform to clothe their dead comrades. Carpenters were busy building pine coffins for the 82 dead. The constant sawing of wood and hammering of nails was torture to those who had lost loved ones. Frances Grummond described the scene:

"One-half of the headquarters building, which was my temporary home, was utilized by carpenters for making pine cases for the dead. I knew that my husband's coffin was being made, and the sound of hammers and the grating of saws was torture to my sensitive nerves." [36]

During the day on Christmas Eve Margaret Carrington spoke with her husband in his office.

"Henry," she began. "I know this may sound crass at a time such as this but what will become of you and your career when the news of this gets out?"

Henry Carrington grimly looked at his wife and responded.

"Margaret, I am in serious trouble. I know of no worse defeat the army has ever suffered at the hands of the hostiles. And as commanding officer I am responsible for this catastrophe! My career is probably over. Oh if only I hadn't given in to Fetterman. I wish I had insisted that he simply relieve the wood train and return as Captain Powell did days before."

Margaret looked at her spouse then and said, "Dear, who heard you give the orders to Captain Fetterman?"

"Just Captain Fetterman," Carrington responded. "No one else was within earshot."

---

36 Ibid, pg 217

"Well then who is to say that you didn't tell Captain Fetterman to simply relieve the wood train and return? After all those were the orders that you consistently gave during our time here. Who is to say that you didn't give them to Captain Fetterman? And he disobeyed the orders that you gave him?"

Carrington looked thunderstruck for a moment. He then said, "My dear you are correct. There is a way to save my career as the only other person to hear those orders is now dead."

On Christmas Day, the burials were made in a trench that had been dug in the frozen ground through back-breaking labor. Two enlisted men were placed in each coffin, while the officers (Brown, Fetterman, and Grummond) rated a separate coffin of their own.

John (Portugee) Philips, meanwhile, had begun to spread word to the army about the disaster that had befallen Fort Phil Kearny. After riding 190 miles through subzero temperatures and snow that was at times 4-5 feet deep, he reached the telegraph station at Horseshoe Station. He handed his dispatches to the operator who furiously typed out a condensed version of what had occurred. (Due to the great length of the dispatches the operator could not type them "verbatim." The effect of the messages sent was thus confusion. No one who received the messages was quite sure what happened although they knew something bad, even terrible, had occurred. But what was it exactly?)

Philips then put on some dry clothing and rode furiously the remaining 40 miles to Fort Laramie. He arrived there at about 11 pm on Christmas Day. His clothing and hair were coated in ice. He slid from his saddle and told the officer of the day that he needed to see the commanding officer.

General Innis N. Palmer was in the midst of a full dress Christmas ball and wasn't pleased by being interrupted by what looked like a walking snowman that had appeared at his grand event.

"What is the meaning of this most impolite interruption," he roared. "And who in blazes are you?"

"Sir, I come from Fort Phil Kearny," Philips responded. "Sir, we have suffered a terrible defeat. Captain Fetterman and his entire command were wiped out in battle four days ago. We need help, Sir."

Philips then handed Palmer the dispatches Carrington had written out. Palmer read them feverously, and then looked up thunderstruck. He asked Philips several more questions, and then began barking orders. Immediately the Christmas ball ended, and officers and non-commissioned officers (sergeants) began making plans for troops to move out at daylight.

Philips was then escorted to his quarters for the evening. He checked on his horse, and was stunned to find out that shortly after he dismounted and reported to General Palmer, his horse simply dropped dead. The exhausting journey and brutal cold had simply been too much for the brave animal.

The following day, no movement was possible, as a howling blizzard prevented any sort of travel. Later that day, a telegram arrived from General Cook in Omaha. Cook had just received one of the abbreviated telegrams regarding the disaster that had occurred at Fort Phil Kearny. Without waiting for all the facts, Cook realized he had to move fast to avert an even bigger catastrophe. He ordered General Palmer to dispatch two companies of cavalry and four companies of infantry, and proceed immediately to Fort Reno and report to Brigadier General Henry Wessels. From there, Wessells would march with the reinforcements to Fort Phil Kearny and relieve Colonel Carrington of his command.

The first good news to reach Fort Phil Kearny since Fetterman arrived in early November, occurred on December 27th. Twenty-five soldiers (three officers and 22 enlisted men) arrived at the front gates from Fort Reno. The officer in charge of this small party was Captain George B. Dandy. He was originally assigned to replace Captain Fred Brown in the quartermaster role. He and his party had arrived at Fort Reno just as the first "garbled" telegram had arrived outlining the disaster that had struck Fort Phil Kearny. Despite the weather and lack of full details, Captain Dandy instantly decided to push onto Fort Phil Kearny.

Upon arrival, Captain Dandy was ushered into Colonel Carrington's office. Dandy snapped a crisp salute and then said; "My god, Colonel what on earth happened?"

Carrington described the horrific demise of Fetterman and his command. He then stated; "Captain let me assure you that I gave Fetterman strict instructions to relieve the wood train and then to return here. He flagrantly disobeyed my orders and the result was the destruction of his entire command."

Dandy sat there stunned. Words were at first hard to come by and then he quietly said, "Colonel, I just can't believe that a modern army could be defeated so badly by Stone Age savages. And that an officer as highly thought of and with the record that Captain Fetterman had would disobey orders. My god sir, it's hard to conceive of."

Carrington said, "Believe it Captain Dandy. Fetterman disobeyed orders and walked into a massive ambush. If he had followed his orders this would never have occurred. And now because of his reckless actions we here are all endangered."

Captain Dandy then asked," Colonel when did you realize that Captain Fetterman was not following your orders? Couldn't you have recalled him?"

Carrington waited before answering. His entire career could be resting on how he answered as he knew there would be an investigation and that Dandy may be questioned.

"Captain, I suppose I could have recalled him or sent an orderly to him asking questions. However, I felt that Captain Fetterman being an experienced officer was carrying out my orders in the manner that he felt was most prudent. Clearly I was mistaken in that manner and I will have to live with that error for the rest of my life."

Captain George Dandy nodded his head and replied, "I see what you are saying Colonel. Clearly you can't try and manage everything. You gave Captain Fetterman orders and the freedom to execute them in the manner that he felt was best. It is tragic that he did what he did but I cannot see anyone faulting you in this situation."

Carrington smiled grimly at Dandy's response. This was exactly what he wanted to hear.

While the fort remained on alert, Jim Bridger, the wily old "mountain man" assured Carrington that there was little or no prospect for a hostile attack. Bridger knew from experience that with the mountains and valleys full of deep snow, the hostiles would "hunker down" in their camps. They wouldn't be going anywhere.

In fact, he was correct and yet incorrect at the same time. No attack materialized, but even with the deep snow the hostiles retreated from the Tongue River territory. The Cheyenne retreated into the Big Horn Mountains, the Arapaho moved to the Yellowstone region and the Sioux scattered into the Powder and Tongue River regions.

On January 3, 1867, Carrington dispatched a report to General Cooke, outlining the disaster and casting all blame for it on Fetterman's blatant disobedience of his orders. There was no one left alive now to contradict Carrington's version of the events.

On January 16, 1867, the long-awaited reinforcements from Fort Laramie, led by Brigadier General Wessels, arrived. It had been a simply grueling journey. The bitter cold and deep snow slowed the column to "a crawl." The food for the horses and mules ran out after 10 days on the march. The animals, crazed with hunger, broke their halters and tried to eat each other's tails and manes. Water ran out, and soldiers found that rivers and creeks were frozen right to the bottom due to the brutal, unrelenting cold. They used axes to cut chunks of ice out of the rivers, and then boiled the ice over fires to create drinking water.

Frances Grummond described the scene as Wessels and his men began marching through the gate: "The bugle call and the long roll were never more gladly echoed in heart. Our spontaneous cry was 'Open wide the gates, and admit our deliverers!' We hardly had patience to don protective outer-garments because of the flow of our quickened blood, and our common outbreak of joy was simply, 'At last! At last! We are saved, we are saved....'"[37]

Along with the reinforcements came the official orders from General Cooke relieving Carrington of command of Fort Phil Kearny.

On January 23, 1867, Carrington, his wife Margaret, the entire headquarters staff, and Frances Grummond, along with an escort of 60 troopers, rode out of Fort Phil Kearny and into the wilds of Wyoming Territory. The temperatures were still well below zero. The covers for the wagons had been doubled, and the fort's carpenters had boarded up the sides and ends of the wagons to keep out the wind. Women and children were huddled in coats, shawls, and all the furs they could find. Frances Grummond, late in her pregnancy, was bitterly cold and feeling every bump as the wagon jolted along over ice and snow. The temperatures inside the wagons, despite the small ovens they kept lit inside, rested at -13 F. After one cavalry trooper had to be pulled from his saddle due to his legs being frozen,

---

[37] Ibid, pg, 224.

A COLD DAY IN HELL

Carrington ordered the legs of the other mounted troopers to be lashed with whips to keep the blood circulating. Coffee that had been boiled over fires and poured into mugs turned into half-frozen slush before the mug was emptied. Bread was so frozen it had to be cut with an ax.

After three days of unbearable suffering, the column reached Fort Reno. There a number of soldiers suffered the agony of the amputation saws as frozen fingers, toes, and even legs were removed.

After three days of relative comfort in the warm quarters of Fort Reno, the expedition set out again towards Fort Casper. It was an uneventful journey (aside from the cold). Upon arrival, Carrington was stunned to find out that his orders had been changed. The 18th Regiment's headquarters had been shifted to Fort McPherson, Nebraska!

So Carrington's expedition struck out again, retracing some of the ground that they had just covered. As the column approached Sage Creek, Carrington's revolver accidentally discharged, wounding him seriously in the thigh. The accompanying surgeons treated the wound and made him comfortable. His column made it to Fort Laramie, where he spent two weeks recovering. From there he traveled by wagon to Fort McPherson. When he arrived there, he was informed that an official board of inquiry would be established to investigate what was becoming known through North America as the "Fetterman Massacre

AFTERMATH

When Colonel Henry Carrington and his column reached Fort McPherson, he was floored to hear that newspapers across North America were full of lurid (and mainly inaccurate) stories of the disaster that had befallen Captain Fetterman and his troops. One New York newspaper correspondent described the battle occurring outside of the gates of Fort Phil Kearny, with Carrington refusing to open the gates to rescue Fetterman's troops! The Commissioner of Indian Affairs, Lewis V. Bogy, claimed Carrington had provoked the Indians into attacking Fetterman's column! When Carrington spoke out and claimed at least three thousand Indians had attacked Fetterman, Bogy publicly ridiculed him. Carrington knew he was now in a battle to save his reputation and his career.

The Sanborn Commission, instituted to discover the facts around the debacle of Fetterman's defeat, first met in Omaha on March 4, 1867. There they took testimony from General Cooke and Lieutenant Bisbee. Bisbee was scathing in his testimony regarding his former commanding officer, and even though he hadn't taken part in the battle (he of course wasn't even at Fort Phil Kearny when the battle occurred), cast all blame for the defeat upon Carrington. Carrington himself gave testimony to the Sanborn Commission in late March 1867. During his testimony, he very carefully and patiently explained his actions from when he received his initial orders to establish Fort Phil Kearny to the battle itself. He went to great pains to explain that he had given Captain Fetterman explicit orders to simply relieve the wood train and return to the fort. He cast all blame for the debacle on Fetterman.

On July 8, 1867, the Sanborn Commission presented its findings. The commission found that "the difficulty in a nutshell was the commanding officer of the district was furnished no more troops or supplies for this state of war than had been provided and furnished him in a state of profound peace. In regions where all was peace, as at Laramie in November, twelve companies were stationed, while in regions where all was war, as at Phil Kearny, there were only five companies allowed." [38]

Carrington had been "officially cleared," but rumors and stories of his alleged lack of courage in dealing with the hostiles continued to filter through the army. The commission dealt Captain Ten Eyck a mild blow when it stated "Ten Eyck moved out and advanced rapidly toward the point from which the sound of firing proceeded, but did not move by so short a route as he might have done..."[39]

Captain Ten Eyck was suffering badly now. With the findings of the Sanborn Commission now public, accounts were spreading that he had been less than aggressive in attempting to rescue Fetterman's command. Ten Eyck truly felt that he had advanced towards Fetterman as quickly as possible. He didn't help his cause by increasing his already heavy drinking. In the late summer of 1867, he was transferred to Fort McPherson, but his drinking continued to escalate. At one point, he arrived for duty so drunk the commanding officer there, Colonel William Dye, pressed charges against him. (Carrington had him arrested for the same offense before the fateful battle. He had subsequently dropped the charges.) When Ten Eyck sobered up, he begged Colonel Dye to withdraw the charges and promised to practice sobriety. Dye withdrew the charges. Ten Eyck promptly "fell off the wagon," and was charged with "conduct unbecoming of an officer and gentleman." A court-martial found him guilty of the charges and ordered him dismissed from the army. Upon reviewing the court-martial findings, however, General Ulysses

---

38 Ibid, pg, 235.

39 Smith, Shannon, "Give Me Eighty men", pg 175.

A COLD DAY IN HELL

Grant took pity on Ten Eyck and ordered the verdict set aside.

For Captain Tenodor Ten Eyck, Grant's mercy couldn't save him. He was haunted by the Fetterman battle and the sights he had seen in the aftermath of it. He continued to drink, and in 1871 he resigned his commission and left the army. He passed away in 1905.

The reader may find it interesting to note that less than a month after the Sanborn Commission presented its' findings, another major battle occurred just outside of Fort Phil Kearny. On August 2, 1867 Captain James Powell was in command of the security detachment guarding a lumber camp. For added security the boxes had been taken off wagons, used to transport the wood. By taking the boxes off the wagons longer pieces of lumber could be piled on the wagons.

The boxes were made of sturdy wood and were strong enough to repel arrows and small arms fire. When they were placed on the ground the walls of the boxes were 2.5 feet tall allowing a soldier to crouch in them and fight from within it. The boxes had been organized into a circular "corral" and the ends of the boxes had been removed allowing movement from box to box.

That day close to 1,000 Sioux led by Red Cloud, struck Captain Powell's command. Powell had 32 men armed with single shot breech loading Springfield rifles. Powell had his men leap into the boxes and began pouring fire into the attacking hostiles. The Sioux were expecting Powell's men to be armed with single shot muskets and knew that all they had to do was "weather the storm" from the first volley or two of the muskets and then they could roll right over the troops. Much to their shock the rate of fire from the troops hunkered down in the boxes didn't slacken. It was a continuous barrage of lead that blasted numerous warriors off their horses. An experienced soldier could fire 12-15 shots per minute with the new breech-loaders. A huge improvement over the old Springfield musket!

As the fighting continued to rage the Sioux began launching flaming arrows into the solder's' mini fortress. They were hoping to ignite the wooden boxes and thus drive the soldiers into the open where they could be slaughtered. Instead all they did was set fire to heaps of dried horse dung, adding clouds of noxious smelling smoke to the already thick clouds of gunpowder smoke hanging over the battlefield.

As the hours of battle continued, Powell had his men who were either wounded or poor shots fall to the rear and act as loaders. The men who were considered the most accurate shots would fire and pass their empty rifle to the rear, while a loaded one was passed forward to them.

Finally after close to four hours of savage, unrelenting combat, reinforcements arrived from Fort Phil Kearny and Red Cloud pulled his warriors back. Powell suffered three killed and less than five wounded. It is estimated that the Sioux suffered well over 100 dead and many more wounded. It was a catastrophic defeat for Red Cloud and the Sioux. It also makes one wonder how the Fetterman battle may have turned out if the troops had been armed with the same breech-loading Springfields as opposed to the single shot muskets that they actually did carry. Considering the carnage created by Wheatley and Fisher with their 16-shot Henry rifles, the battle may have very well turned out quite different!

Henry Carrington left the army in 1870 and became a Professor of Military Science at Wabash College in Indiana. That same year his wife Margaret died of tuberculosis. Frances Grummond, who had returned home to Tennessee, sent a letter of condolence to Henry and they began to correspond and then married in 1871. In July 1908 the Carringtons and other survivors returned to the site of Fort Phil Kearny, where a memorial was being established. The fort itself had been abandoned in 1868 when the US government agreed to withdraw military forces from the Bozeman Trail region under the terms of the Fort Laramie treaty. Almost as soon as the last soldier marched out of the gates of Fort Phil Kearny, Cheyenne and Sioux warriors rushed in and burnt the post to the ground.

Frances and Henry Carrington walked the grounds of their former post. Little remained of it. There were a few signs of the former foundation, but that was about it. Carrington gave an hour-long speech to the crowd gathered to see the memorial. In his speech, he defended his actions at Fort Phil Kearny and continued to cast blame for the crushing defeat upon Captain Fetterman. He did, however, absolve Captain Ten Eyck of any blame in so far as failing to move as quickly as possible to Fetterman's aid.

Henry Carrington passed away in 1912 at the age of 88. Frances had preceded him in death in 1911.

Since the battle ended, the accepted account was that William Fetterman disobeyed direct orders from Henry Carrington and led his command to disaster. In the early 20th century, a story began "making the rounds" that Fetterman had boasted "Give me eighty good men and I'll ride through the whole Sioux nation." It appears odd that this came out over 30 years after the battle, and outside of the Carringtons, no other survivors from Fort Phil Kearny could remember Fetterman saying that.

So one must ask – is the traditional account of the Fetterman battle accurate? That is, did he disobey orders? Upon looking at the evidence, the answer appears clear. And that is that Captain William Fetterman did not disobey orders.

The main evidence for this statement is the fact that when Fetterman led his command out of Fort Phil Kearny, he swung northeast, as opposed to west where the wood-train was situated. If Colonel Carrington had indeed given direct orders to Fetterman to relieve the wood train why did he not immediately send messengers to

Fetterman inquiring as to what he was doing? Carrington was adamant during his testimony before the Sanborn Commission and in later writings that he had given Fetterman strict orders to relieve the wood train and return to the fort. Again, if this was what actually occurred why did he not attempt to recall Fetterman when it became immediately clear that Fetterman was not proceeding to the relief of the wood train? Certainly there was ample time for Carrington to send a messenger to Fetterman before Fetterman became embroiled in battle. One must imagine that an officer as cautious and prudent as Carrington and as concerned as he was about the vulnerability of his command, would have reacted very quickly to the sight of his direct orders being disobeyed and as such would have attempted to recall Fetterman. And yet he did not.

Another thing that must be considered is that Captain Fetterman, unlike Lieutenant George Grummond, had no history whatsoever of disobeying orders from his superiors. By all accounts, Fetterman was an aggressive, yet intelligent and prudent officer. During the Civil War, he had never disobeyed orders while leading his troops aggressively and intelligently. Indeed one does not reach senior rank in a modern military by disobeying orders. Thus why would he have done so at this time? Is it reasonable to suggest that William Fetterman would have put his career at risk by disobeying a direct order from his superior? That same superior whom he was to replace in less than a month? The evidence suggests not.

No soldier who marched out the gates of Fort Phil Kearny on that bitterly cold December morning lived to tell the tale of what transpired between Fetterman, Grummond, and the rest of the troops. All one can do is decide what probably occurred, based on the historical evidence. That evidence is that Captain William Fetterman was given orders by Colonel Henry Carrington to strike the hostiles. Fetterman marched out of the fort and proceeded in a direction which clearly indicated he was not relieving the wood train – he was attempting to strike the hostiles. Colonel Carrington made no attempt to recall him. We know the cavalry led by Lieutenant George Grummond preceded Fetterman into the ambush zone. Grummond's military career indicated a history of blindly disobeying orders and recklessly charging into battles. It stands to reason that Grummond, who had done exactly that just two weeks earlier, proceeded in the same fashion on December 21, 1866. That left Captain William Fetterman in a terrible position. Does he abandon Grummond's command to its fate or does he proceed into battle with young inexperienced troops armed with obsolete weapons in an attempt to rescue Grummond's troops? William Fetterman made the honorable decision and attempted to rescue his comrades. It proved to be fruitless, and cost Fetterman and every soldier with him their lives. But it doesn't detract from the incredible bravery displayed by those soldiers.

Colonel Henry Carrington "rolled the dice" and lost that icy cold day in December 1866. He turned loose the best weapon that he had, and his best was out-numbered and out-fought at the end. At that point, he scrambled to save his own reputation and career.

Captain William Fetterman and the 82 men who marched through the gates of Fort Phil Kearny on December 21, 1866, upheld the highest tradition of the United States Army and should be remembered as such.

BIBLIOGRAPHY

I. Brown, Dee, *The Fetterman Massacre* London, Pan Books, Ltd., 1974.

II. *California Military Museum,* Retrieved from: http://www.military.museum.org/Conner.html, Major General Patrick Edward Connor,

III. Carrington, Margaret *Absaraka, Home of the Crows,* Chicago,: R.R. Donnelley and Sons, 1950.

Murray, Robert "Military Posts in the Powder River Country of Wyoming, 1865-1894," University of Nebraska Press, Lincoln, 1968.

Smith, Shannon, Give Me Eighty Men, Women and the Myth of the Fetterman Fight, Lincoln, University of Nebraska Press, 2008.

IV. US Congress, 50th, 1st sess. Senate executive document.

US War Dept., The War of the Rebellion…Official Records, Ser I, Vol 38, Pt I.

ABOUT THE AUTHOR

CRAIG WALLACE

Craig Wallace was born and raised in Toronto, Ontario. He graduated from the University of Western Ontario in 1987 with a degree in history. He is the author of "A Slip in the Rain, the True Story of the 1967-72 Toronto Argonauts and the Fumble that Killed Canada's Team", "The Forgotten Summit, A Canadian Perspective on the 1974 Canada Soviet Hockey Series", and "Into the Valley of Death". The latter is an account of the 1876 Little Big Horn battle. He currently lives in Hamilton, Ontario and can be reached at craigwallace@bell.net.